CW01508741

The Power of Empathy and Emotional Validation

From Conflict to Connection: Your Path to Meaningful Relationships

Daniel Brooks

Chapter Zero

Chapter Zero LLC
16192 Coastal Highway
Lewes, 19958
Delaware – USA
Contact: info@chapterzerobooks.com

Disclaimer: The information provided in this book is for informational purposes only. While every effort has been made to ensure the accuracy and completeness of the information contained herein, the author and publisher make no warranties or representations, express or implied, regarding the contents of this book. This book is intended to inform and inspire, but it is not a substitute for professional advice or therapy. The author and publisher disclaim any liability arising directly or indirectly from the use or application of any of the contents of this book. Always consult with a qualified professional before making any decisions related to the topics discussed in this book.

Paperback ISBN 978-1-961963-05-4
Hardcover ISBN 978-1-961963-06-1

Contents

Connection:

The power that exists
between people when they
feel seen, heard, and valued.
— Brené Brown

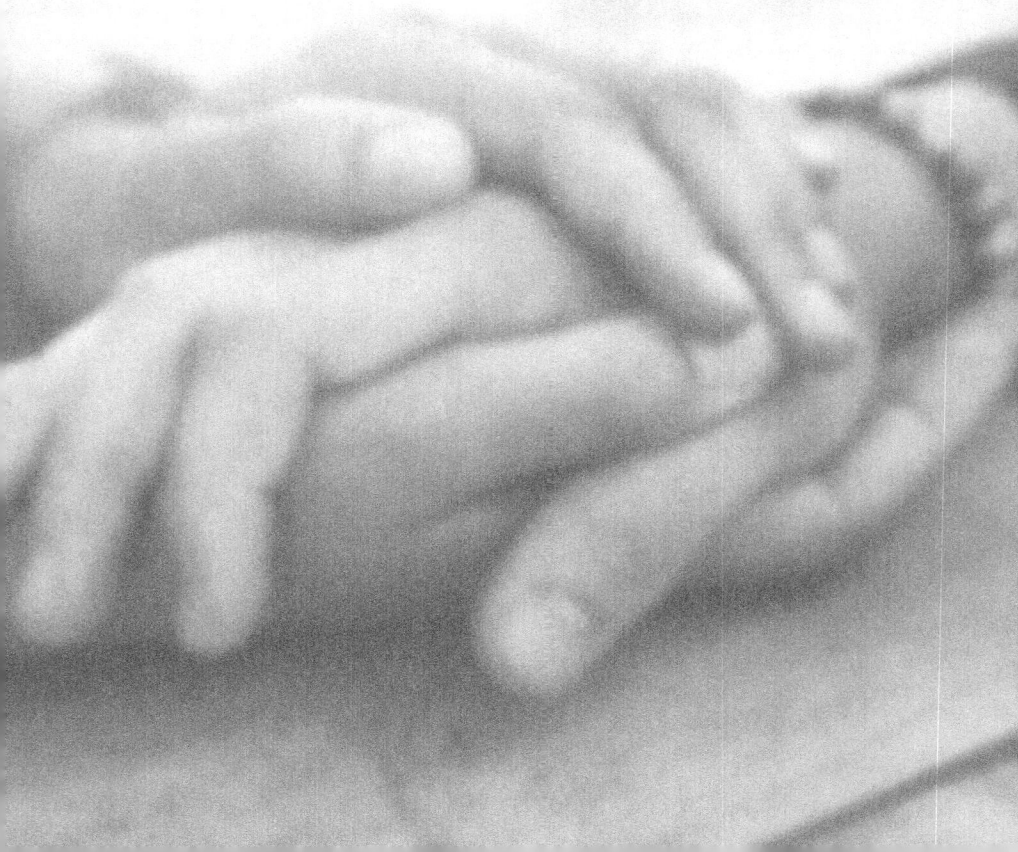

Introduction

Do you ever feel like your relationships are missing something, and you're not sure what that something is?

If so, you're not alone. The good news is that authentic bonds are possible through cultivating two simple but profound skills – empathy and emotional validation.

The ability to understand and share another person's feelings, to truly step into their shoes and see the world through their eyes, is the essence of empathy. On the other hand, we have emotional validation, which is the practice of letting others know that their feelings are valid, natural, and important. Both of these skills can drastically transform our relationships, drawing us closer to those around us and cultivating environments of trust, respect, and deep connections.

Imagine being in a room full of strangers, each person engrossed in their world, disconnected and distant. But then, there's a shift. Someone reaches out, genuinely interested in understanding you. They actively listen, acknowledge your experiences, and suddenly, that room doesn't feel so vast and cold anymore. You can say that there's warmth, a connection, and a bridge is formed. Actually, all of this is the power of empathy and emotional validation.

In our fast-paced digital age, we're more connected than ever. And yet, ironically, genuine connections seem harder to forge. The "how are you?" greetings often feel superficial, and in-depth, vulnerable conversations sometimes seem like relics of the past. How, then, do we reclaim and nurture these invaluable human connections? That's what we'll explore throughout this book.

As a counselor and communication expert, I've had the privilege to witness countless moments of transformation. Once, a young man came to me, shoulders slumped, voice barely audible, explaining how he felt perpetually misunderstood by his family. Over several sessions, as we worked on enhancing his communication skills and fostering empathy, a miraculous change occurred. The same young man walked in one day, shoulders back, a light in his eyes, sharing a heartwarming tale of a recent family dinner. A dinner where they laughed, shared, and, most importantly, *understood* each other. This wasn't magic. It was the power of empathy and emotional validation in action. In fact, a little empathy goes a long way.

Throughout this comprehensive guide, we'll explore various facets of these concepts:

- The historical, psychological, and neurological foundations of empathy, as well as its various types and pivotal role in human interactions.

- The transformative power of emotional validation, looking into its psychology and how it can have a significant impact on our well-being.

- Techniques to enhance communication and strategies for navigating both personal relationships and professional landscapes with empathy and validation.

- Addressing modern challenges, including the digital realm and how empathy plays out in online interactions.

- Tackling societal, cultural, and personal barriers that might impede our capacity for genuine connection.

To ensure a holistic learning experience and a practical application, each chapter concludes with real-life practice scenarios, exercises, and reflection points. These are carefully designed to help you internalize the content, providing a hands-on approach to mastering the art of empathy and emotional validation.

In sharing my experiences as a counselor and communication expert, I hope to illustrate the profound impact these skills can have. This is no textbook filled with academic jargon but a practical toolkit filled with actionable insights to bring more meaning and joy to your relationships.

So how do we get there? How can we create a world where people are more generous with their listening and empathy? More open to understanding different perspectives? The journey begins here. Through listening, empathy, and openness, together, we can build bridges to the heart of human connection. In this book, you will find out everything. Grab your favorite comfy chair and a hot cup of tea - you have an inspiring adventure ahead!

Chapter One

Foundations of Empathy

I n this chapter, we will lay the groundwork for understanding the complex and transformative power of empathy. We'll explore the historical and psychological perspectives that have shaped our understanding of empathy, explore the fascinating neuroscience behind how our brains connect with others, and differentiate between the types of empathy: cognitive, emotional, and compassionate. We'll also discuss the profound benefits of cultivating empathy in our daily interactions. To help you apply these concepts, we'll examine a real-life scenario and provide exercises and reflection points for you to practice. This chapter aims to provide a comprehensive understanding of empathy, setting the stage for the rest of our journey.

Historical and Psychological Perspectives on Empathy

Empathy, as a term and a concept, has a rich history intertwined with various fields of study, including philosophy, psychology, and neuroscience.

The term "empathy" originated from the German word "Einfühlung," which translates to "feeling into." It was first introduced in the late 19th century by German philosopher Robert Vischer as a means of describing our emotional connection to art. However, the concept of empathy extends far beyond this initial definition, permeating our understanding of human relationships and emotional experiences.

In the realm of psychology, empathy has been a subject of interest for over a century. Early psychologists like Edward Titchener and Carl Rogers significantly contributed to our understanding of empathy. In the early 20th century, Titchener was the first to translate "Einfühlung" to "empathy" in English, defining it as the ability to project oneself into another's perspective.

Carl Rogers, a prominent figure in humanistic psychology, later expanded on this concept in the mid-20th century. He defined empathy as a core component of effective psychotherapy. According to Rogers, empathy involves understanding the client's feelings and perspectives without losing the as-if condition, meaning the therapist maintains their separate identity while understanding the client's experiences as if they were their own.

Modern psychology continues to explore empathy, recognizing it as a complex, multifaceted phenomenon. It's regarded as an essential element of emotional intelligence, a key factor in successful interpersonal relationships, and a crucial component of prosocial behavior.

From a neuroscientific perspective, the discovery of mirror neurons in the late 20th century provided a biological basis for empathy. These neurons, found in the premotor cortex and the posterior parietal cortex of the brain, fire both when we perform an action and when we observe someone else performing the same action. This mirroring mechanism is thought to underlie our ability to understand and share others' emotions, providing a neural foundation for empathy.

Understanding the historical and psychological perspectives on empathy allows us to appreciate its complexity and its integral role in human connection.

The Neuroscience of Empathy: How Our Brains Connect

As we continue our exploration of empathy, we find ourselves at the intersection of psychology and biology. It's here that we uncover the intricate neural processes that enable us to connect with others on a deeply emotional level. The field of neuroscience has helped uncover how our nervous system makes empathy possible. Studying the biology of the brain has revealed some incredible insights into why we can understand each other on such a fundamental human level.

Central to our understanding of empathy from a neurological perspective is the concept of mirror neurons. These specialized brain cells respond both when we perform an action and when we observe someone else performing the same action. Picture yourself watching someone else enjoy a slice of their favorite cake. Even though you're not the one eating, you might find yourself experiencing a hint of their delight. This vicarious experience is your mirror neuron system in action.

Mirror neurons were first identified in the 1990s in macaque monkeys and have since been found in humans. They are primarily located in the premotor cortex, which is involved in planning and executing movements, and the posterior parietal cortex, which processes sensory information and coordinates responses. When these neurons 'mirror' the actions or emotions of others, they provide a direct neural pathway for understanding other people's experiences.

This mirroring process is believed to be a fundamental mechanism underlying empathy. When we witness someone else expressing an emotion, such as joy or sadness, our mirror neurons for that emotion activate, creating a subtle echo of their feeling in our minds. This allows us to 'feel into' others and understand their emotional states intuitively.

However, this process is not just a simple act of mimicry. Our brains are continuously integrating and interpreting this mirrored information in the context of our own experiences and knowledge. This allows us to understand not just what the other person is feeling but also why they might be feeling that way.

Here's an encouraging thing about empathy - it's not necessarily set in stone. Studies have found our ability to empathize is actually kind of like a muscle. It can grow stronger when we exercise it regularly. Activities that promote mindfulness and compassion, such as meditation, have been found to enhance the brain's empathetic responses. This speaks to the remarkable plasticity of our brains — their ability to change and adapt in response to experiences.

Understanding the neuroscience of empathy deepens our appreciation of our inherent capacity for connection. It underscores that empathy is not just a social or psychological phenomenon but also a biological one, deeply rooted in our neural circuits. As we further explore the different facets of empathy, remember that this ability to connect, to truly understand others, is part of who we are, right down to our neurons.

Differentiating types of empathy: Cognitive, emotional, and Compassionate

In understanding empathy, we must recognize the different types that play distinct roles in our interactions with others. Let's delve into the three primary types of empathy: cognitive, emotional, and compassionate.

Cognitive Empathy

As human beings, we all possess the ability to empathize with others. Yet, not all empathy looks and feels the same. Cognitive empathy, for example, is one type of empathy that often gets overlooked or misunderstood.

Cognitive empathy is the ability to understand someone else's perspective or situation on a cognitive level. This means that we can acknowledge and appreciate another person's thoughts, emotions, and experiences without necessarily feeling them ourselves. In other words, we can recognize that someone else is feeling sad, angry, or happy, even if we don't feel those emotions ourselves.

For some people, cognitive empathy comes naturally. They may be able to read between the lines of someone's words or body language to understand what they're really feeling. Others, however, may struggle with cognitive empathy, especially if their own emotions and experiences are clouding their ability to see things from another person's point of view.

So, why is cognitive empathy important? First and foremost, it helps us connect with others. When we can understand where someone else is coming from, we can communicate with them in a way that is more compassionate and meaningful. Furthermore, cognitive empathy can help us resolve conflicts and build stronger relationships. It allows us to see beyond our own biases and assumptions and get to the heart of what someone else is experiencing.

However, it's important to note that cognitive empathy is only one piece of the empathy puzzle. To truly connect with others, it's essential to tap into emotional empathy and practice compassionate empathy. Emotional empathy involves actually feeling someone else's emotions, while compassionate empathy consists in taking action to help or support someone based on our understanding of their situation.

Emotional Empathy

Emotional empathy is a powerful force that allows us to step into someone else's emotional shoes and experience their feelings as if they were our own. It's like diving headfirst into a pool of emotions, immersing ourselves in the depths of another person's joys, sorrows, and everything in between.

When we tap into emotional empathy, we bridge the gap between ourselves and others, forging a profound connection that transcends words. We don't just understand how someone feels; we feel it in the depths of our being. It's as if their emotions flow through our veins, intertwining with our own thoughts and experiences.

But let me tell you, emotional empathy can be both a gift and a burden. On the one hand, it allows us to offer genuine comfort and support to those who are hurting. We can sit beside someone in their darkest moments and say, "I understand. I feel your pain." It's an invitation for them to open up, to be vulnerable because they know they're not alone in what they are going through.

Yet, on the other hand, emotional empathy can sometimes be overwhelming. When we absorb the emotions of others, it can be difficult to differentiate between what we're feeling and what they're feeling. We become sponges, soaking up the intensity of their emotions, sometimes at the expense of our own well-being. It's as if we carry the weight of the world on our shoulders, never fully able to shake off the heaviness.

But here's the thing about emotional empathy: it's a superpower that requires practice, self-awareness, and boundaries! We must learn to discern between our own emotions and those of others. We need to ask ourselves, "Is this feeling mine, or am I picking up on someone else's energy?" It's like untangling a web of emotions, carefully sorting through the threads to find our truth.

And yet, even with practice, emotional empathy can still surprise us. It can catch us off guard, like a sudden rainstorm on a sunny day, leaving us drenched and bewildered. We may find ourselves overwhelmed by the intensity of someone else's pain or overcome with joy in their moments of triumph. It's in these moments that we truly realize the depth of our emotional capacity, the vastness of our empathetic hearts.

Therefore, I invite you to ponder emotional empathy. Reflect on your experiences of feeling deeply connected to others, on the times when someone else's emotions enveloped your being. What did you learn from those moments? How did they shape your understanding of yourself and the world around you?

Let me clarify something here; emotional empathy is not just about feeling FOR others; it's about feeling WITH others. It's an acknowledgment of our shared humanity, a reminder that we are all in this journey called life together.

Compassionate Empathy

Compassionate empathy, a form of empathy that goes beyond just understanding or sharing in another person's emotions, basically means actively seeking to assist or alleviate the discomfort experienced by another. It combines cognitive and emotional empathy, bringing together understanding, feeling, and action.

When you engage in compassionate empathy, it's as though you're stepping beyond the invisible boundary that separates you from others, stepping into their space, not just to understand or share their feelings but to bring relief, comfort, or solutions where possible. You don't merely sympathize from the sidelines, but you mobilize your resources and energy to help.

Picture a situation in which a friend has lost their job. Cognitive empathy allows you to understand the worry your friend is experiencing due to this sudden change. Emotional empathy enables you to feel the same concern and fear, mirroring their feelings. However, compassionate empathy will drive you to go a step further. You might help your friend revise their resume, connect them with job opportunities in your network, or simply be there to listen and provide moral support throughout their job search.

We can say that compassionate empathy is the core of human connection, the action-oriented facet of empathy that fuels acts of kindness, big or small. It's the driving force behind every community service project, each volunteer at a food bank, every mentor guiding a mentee, and the comforting shoulder offered during tough times.

However, there's a cautionary note to be heeded here. While compassionate empathy can be deeply rewarding, it's essential to ensure your own emotional well-being is not compromised. Just as flight attendants instruct us to secure our oxygen masks before helping others, the same principle applies to compassionate empathy. When helping others, it's vital not to neglect your needs or deplete your resources.

To practice compassionate empathy responsibly, cultivate an awareness of your emotional state. Monitor your energy levels and ensure you're not constantly draining your reserves without taking the time to recharge. You might establish a routine that includes self-care activities or develop a support system that helps you maintain balance.

By offering compassionate empathy, you're not just validating someone's emotions; you're also proactively participating in their emotional narrative, offering solace and support. It's about practicing humanity at its best: recognizing and responding to the needs of others in a way that is both understanding and proactive.

These three types of empathy work together to form our empathetic abilities. Cognitive empathy lays the foundation for understanding, emotional empathy creates emotional connections, and compassionate empathy drives us to take meaningful actions to support others.

The Benefits of Cultivating Empathy in Daily Interactions

As we navigate through our daily lives, we constantly interact with others, each interaction presenting an opportunity to connect, understand, and empathize. Cultivating empathy is not just about enhancing our relationships; it's about enriching our lives and the lives of those around us. Empathy allows us to step outside our own experiences and view the world from another's perspective. It's a skill that, when practiced regularly, can bring about profound benefits in our daily interactions. Let's explore these benefits in more detail.

1. **Improved Relationships:** Empathy forms the bedrock of meaningful relationships. When we empathize with others, we demonstrate that we value their feelings and experiences. This promotes mutual respect and understanding, strengthening our connections with family, friends, and colleagues.

2. **Effective Communication:** Empathy improves our communication skills. It allows us to listen actively and respond thoughtfully, facilitating open and honest dialogues. For instance, when a friend shares a concern, empathizing can help us respond in a way that acknowledges their feelings rather than offering unsolicited advice.

3. **Conflict Resolution:** Empathy can really help with resolving conflicts. By understanding the other person's perspective, we can address disagreements in a more constructive manner, which means instead of focusing on who's right or wrong, empathy guides us toward finding common ground and mutual solutions.

4. **Emotional Well-being:** Practicing empathy contributes to our emotional well-being. It encourages positive emotions like compassion and kindness while also helping us manage negative emotions. When we empathize with someone's struggles, we realize that we're not alone in our experiences, which can be comforting during difficult times.

5. **Increased Tolerance and Understanding:** Empathy broadens our horizons and improves tolerance. It helps us appreciate diverse perspectives and experiences, reducing prejudices and biases. Empathizing with a coworker from a different cultural background, for example, can help us understand their customs and values, thereby creating a more inclusive environment.

6. **Leadership Skills:** Empathy is a key leadership skill. Leaders who empathize can understand their team's needs and motivations better, leading to more effective management strategies. They can build a supportive work environment where everyone feels valued and heard.

Cultivating empathy is like planting a seed - it requires patience, care, and time. But the fruits it bears are manifold, enriching our daily interactions and experiences. As we continue to nurture this skill, we'll find our world becoming a little more understanding, a little more connected, and a lot more compassionate.

Practice Scenario: A Moment of Misunderstanding Between Two Friends

Let's consider a scenario involving two friends, Lisa and Sarah. They've been friends since high school, sharing countless memories and experiences. However, recently, they've hit a rough patch.

Sarah has been going through a tough time at work. She's been feeling overwhelmed and stressed, and one day, she decides to confide in Lisa about her struggles. However, instead of the comfort she was hoping for, Sarah feels dismissed when Lisa quickly brushes off her concerns, saying, "Everyone has work stress, Sarah. You just need to toughen up."

This response leaves Sarah feeling invalidated and misunderstood. She was seeking empathy and understanding, but instead, she felt judged and belittled. This moment of misunderstanding creates a rift in their friendship, leaving both of them feeling disconnected.

Now, imagine if Lisa had responded with empathy. If, instead of dismissing Sarah's feelings, she had said, "I can see you're really stressed, Sarah. I'm sorry you're going through this. Want to talk more about it?" This empathetic response would have made Sarah feel heard and understood, strengthening their bond instead of straining it.

Exercises and Reflection Points

Remember to use a notebook to write down your answers to these exercises and a journal to reflect on the situation. This active engagement will help you internalize the concept of empathy and apply it in your daily life.

Exercises:

1. Empathetic Response Exercise: Reflect on the scenario above. Write down three alternative responses Lisa could have given that would demonstrate empathy toward Sarah. Remember, an empathetic response acknowledges the other person's feelings and shows understanding.

2. Role Reversal Exercise: Put yourself in Sarah's shoes. How would you feel if you were in her situation? Now, switch roles and imagine being Lisa. How could you have handled the situation differently? Write down your thoughts.

3. Daily Empathy Practice: For the next week, consciously practice empathy in your daily interactions. It could be with a family member, a friend, or a colleague. Take note of these interactions and how empathy changes the dynamics of the conversation.

Reflection Points:

1. Understanding Empathy: Reflect on how empathy (or lack thereof) impacted Lisa and Sarah's friendship. How do you think their relationship might change if they continue to lack empathy in their interactions?

2. Personal Reflection: Can you remember when you were in a similar situation to Lisa or Sarah? How did you respond? How do you wish you had responded?

3. The Power of Empathy: Reflect on the potential of empathy to transform relationships. How can practicing empathy benefit your personal and professional relationships?

My Notes

Chapter Two

The Transformative Nature of Validation

As we turn the page to the next chapter of our journey, we encounter a concept as powerful as empathy - emotional validation. This process of acknowledging and accepting another person's emotional experiences can be a catalyst for profound transformation. It's a tool that, when employed with care and understanding, can strengthen our relationships, improve our communication, and significantly contribute to our overall well-being.

As a counselor, I've witnessed the transformative power of validation and how it can help individuals feel heard, understood, and valued. In this chapter, we'll unravel the psychology behind feeling acknowledged, distinguish genuine validation from superficial acknowledgments, and discuss the potential harm of invalidation. We'll also provide practical steps to practice and provide genuine validation. Through real-life scenarios and reflective exercises, we'll learn how to incorporate emotional validation into our daily interactions, fostering deeper connections and more meaningful interactions.

The Psychology of Feeling Acknowledged

The human psyche is complex and multifaceted, with a myriad of factors contributing to our overall well-being. One such factor, often overlooked, is the feeling of being acknowledged. When our emotions and what we've been through are seen and accepted, it's huge for our mental health. Having our feelings and experiences validated instead of ignored or rejected makes a big difference. It can be healing when someone truly gets what we're going through on the inside.

When we feel acknowledged, it's as if a spotlight is cast on our inner world. Our feelings, thoughts, and experiences are brought to the forefront, recognized, and validated. This recognition sends a powerful message – our emotions are valid, real, and important. This can have a profound impact on our self-perception and self-esteem. We start to view our emotions as valid and important, which in turn fosters a sense of self-worth and confidence.

In my counseling practice, I've seen the transformative power of feeling acknowledged. I recall a client, let's call her Jane, who came to me with a heavy heart. She was going through a difficult breakup and was struggling with feelings of loneliness and sadness. However, what compounded her distress was the lack of validation she felt from her friends. They would often dismiss her feelings, telling her to "move on" or "just be happy." This dismissal made Jane feel isolated and misunderstood.

In our sessions, I made it a point to acknowledge Jane's feelings. I would say things like, "It sounds like you're feeling really lonely right now," or "It must be tough dealing with such intense sadness."

This simple act of validation had a profound impact on Jane. She reported feeling seen and understood, which in turn helped her process her emotions more effectively. I remember well that in our last session, Jane told me that, over time, she had noticed a significant improvement in her emotional well-being.

On the flip side, when our feelings are dismissed or invalidated, it can lead to a host of negative psychological effects. We may start to question the validity of our emotions, leading to self-doubt and confusion. This can erode our self-esteem and can also give rise to feelings of loneliness and isolation. In some cases, chronic invalidation can even contribute to mental health issues such as anxiety and depression.

Getting validation about our feelings goes way beyond just making us feel better mentally. It actually improves all kinds of areas in life. When someone really acknowledges what you re going through, you're more likely to open up and share honestly with them and others too. That leads to stronger bonds and deeper connections. Plus, you get more comfortable expressing yourself and what you need, which leads to healthier relationships that feel more fulfilling. Basically, when people take the time to understand you, it allows you to connect better all around. The impact starts internally but then ripples out, making your interactions, relationships, and overall quality of life better.

Distinguishing Genuine Validation from Superficial Acknowledgments

Understanding emotional validation involves recognizing the difference between genuine validation and superficial acknowledgments. While these two forms of recognition might appear similar, they vary significantly in their depth, intent, and impact.

But you may ask, what is superficial acknowledgment exactly? Superficial acknowledgment is often a brief, passing response to someone's feelings or experiences. It's the "I see" or "I hear you" that we might offer during conversations.

Should a friend discuss a work project concern with you, a cursory response could be, "That sounds tough, but I'm sure you'll figure it out." While not necessarily harmful, it lacks the depth and understanding that genuine validation provides. It acknowledges the situation but doesn't truly validate the emotions involved.

Genuine validation, on the other hand, is a deeper, more meaningful acknowledgment of another's emotional experience. It's not just about hearing; it's about understanding. It involves empathetically stepping into the other person's shoes and seeing the world from their perspective. It's an affirmation that their feelings are real, valid, and important. For example, in response to the same friend sharing concerns about a work project, a genuine validation could be, "It sounds like this project is causing you a lot of stress. It's understandable that you're feeling overwhelmed."

Consider the experience of a woman named Emily. Emily was dealing with significant stress about her job. When she tried to express her worries to her friends, they often responded with comments like, "Don't worry, it'll be fine" or "Just relax, you're overthinking." These responses were superficial acknowledgments that dismissed Emily's feelings rather than validating them.

When Emily shared her concerns with her partner, she experienced a different kind of response. Instead of dismissing her stress, her partner would say things like, "It sounds like you're feeling really stressed about your job. That must be hard for you." This response acknowledged Emily's feelings without judgment or dismissal. It made her feel seen and understood, which in turn helped her manage her stress more effectively.

During my professional life, I've seen how this kind of genuine validation can transform a person's ability to open up and cope with stress and anxiety. For example, I had a client who was overwhelmed with work and family demands. By listening and reflecting back that it's totally understandable she feels burned out and frustrated, it allowed her to open up more about what she was going through internally. Our communication improved, she felt comfortable asking for support, and her anxiety decreased over time.

The point is genuine validation enhances relationships, communication, and overall wellness. As we explore this topic more, I will share specific tips for validating others' emotions in everyday life.

The Dangers of Invalidation and Minimizing Others' Feelings

When we navigate the world of human emotions, one of the most harmful actions we can take is to invalidate or minimize the feelings of others. Invalidation is a dismissal or rejection of someone's emotional experience while minimizing is a downplaying of the intensity or importance of their feelings. Both actions can have a profound negative impact on the individual and the relationship.

Here are some of the dangers associated with invalidation and minimizing others' feelings:

- *Erosion of Trust and Connection:* Having your feelings constantly invalidated or minimized can really damage trust and closeness in a relationship over time. For example, say Clara opens up to her friend about some scary health symptoms she's having. But her friend responds, "Oh, Clara, you always think something's wrong with you!" Even though the friend means well, comments like that make Clara feel totally dismissed. She ends up feeling misunderstood and like she can't share vulnerable stuff with that person. When things like that happen repeatedly, people start withdrawing from the relationship, and the connection fades. Clara may open up less and less because her feelings keep getting invalidated. The point is that constantly minimizing or rejecting someone's emotions wears away at the bond gradually. People need to know their feelings will be heard and accepted, not shrugged off or belittled.

- *Increased Emotional Distress:* When people's emotions are shut down or brushed off, it often makes them feel even worse emotionally. If someone's already upset about something, being told they're overreacting or shouldn't feel that way tends to make the distress even more intense. For example, say a guy is super anxious about a job interview. But his partner tells him, "Don't be so nervous. Just relax!" Even though it's meant to help, it just makes his anxiety skyrocket even more. Now instead of feeling understood, he feels totally alone in his stress. Invalidating people's emotions dismisses their feelings at the very moment they need support. It heightens emotional pain rather than lessening it. What people need is to feel heard and validated, not have their emotions rejected or minimized.

- *Self-Doubt and Confusion*: Having your emotions constantly shut down can definitely lead to self-doubt and confusion. When someone tells you your feelings are wrong or not important, you start to second-guess your own reactions. To give you an idea, say a teenager is really disappointed she didn't make the soccer team. But her parent brushes it off, saying, "It's not a big deal. Try again next year." Even though she feels crushed, comments like that make her wonder if she's overreacting and being too sensitive. And you know what happens? Over time, dealing with that kind of invalidation can make you distrust your own emotions. You start questioning if your feelings are valid or if you're making too much of things. It's really damaging to be told your emotional responses are wrong or irrational when they're perfectly normal.

- *Suppression of Emotions*: Consistent invalidation and minimizing can lead individuals to suppress their emotions. When people's feelings keep getting shut down or minimized, it can definitely lead them to start suppressing their emotions. If your reactions are constantly invalidated, after a while, you start to feel it's not safe to open up and share how you really feel. For example, I've worked with guys who always heard "Don't be so sensitive!" anytime they showed emotion growing up. Over time, they learned to just shove their feelings down and keep quiet. Always having your feelings belittled like that can cause serious emotional and mental health problems later on. People need to feel safe expressing themselves without being invalidated or made to feel bad about it.

Understanding these dangers is a crucial step in practicing emotional validation. It helps us become more mindful of our responses and strive to provide genuine validation that supports and uplifts others.

Steps to Avoid Invalidation and Provide Genuine Validation

As we learn about understanding and practicing emotional validation, we must also learn how to avoid invalidation. Invalidation, whether intentional or not, can create emotional distance and cause harm. On the other hand, genuine validation can bridge gaps, heal wounds, and deepen our connections. So how can we get better at validating instead of invalidating? Here are some tips that can help:

1. *Active Listening*: Active listening is more than just hearing the words that are spoken. It's about being fully present in the conversation, absorbing the information, and responding thoughtfully. This involves not only listening to the words but also paying attention to the emotions behind them. If your friend is expressing her frustration about a work situation, active listening means putting aside your phone, maintaining eye contact, and responding with understanding, such as, "That sounds really challenging; I can see why you're frustrated."

2. *Empathetic Responses*: Empathy is the ability to understand and share the feelings of another. It's about more than

just recognizing someone else's emotions; it's about feeling them on a personal level and responding in a way that communicates that understanding. For example, if your brother shares his disappointment about a missed promotion, an empathetic response could be, "I can see why you're disappointed. You worked so hard for this. It's completely natural to feel this way."

3. *Non-Verbal Cues*: Our body language can speak volumes about our level of engagement and empathy. Maintaining eye contact, nodding in understanding, and leaning in slightly can all signal to the other person that we are present and attentive to their feelings. For instance, if your friend is sharing his worries about his upcoming move, maintaining eye contact and nodding as he speaks can show him that you're genuinely interested and empathetic to his situation. On the other hand, crossed arms, lack of eye contact, or constantly checking your phone can send a message of disinterest or dismissal, which can feel invalidating. Facial expressions also play a crucial role in validation. A concerned look when someone is sharing a problem, a smile when they share something positive, or a calm and neutral expression when they're sharing something difficult can all help to validate their feelings. Silence, too, can be a powerful non-verbal cue. Sometimes, what a person needs most is not advice or solutions but simply a quiet space to express their feelings. By providing that space, you're validating their need to be heard. All these little physical cues signal that it's okay for someone to communicate honestly and be vulnerable. It encourages more open, meaningful dialogue when people feel fully heard and affirmed through your

body language.

4. *Avoid Judgmental Language*: The words we choose really affect our connections with others. Using judgmental phrases like "You're overreacting" or "It's not that big of a deal" can invalidate someone's feelings and experiences and make them feel shut down. When you speak in a validating manner, you can make someone feel truly heard and accepted. For example, saying things like 'I get why you're so upset.' This matters to you, and it makes complete sense you feel this way" shows you're not dismissing their experience. Validating language is all about really acknowledging the emotion behind what someone is going through rather than judging or downplaying it. It demonstrates you empathize with where they're coming from.

5. *Ask Open-Ended Questions*: Asking open-ended questions is a great way to show interest in someone's feelings and get a deeper understanding of their experience. Closed questions that can be answered in just a word or two, like "Are you okay?" don't really encourage the person to open up. But when you ask an open question like "How are you feeling about this?" or "What was that like for you?", it invites them to share a fuller, more thoughtful response. Those types of questions demonstrate you genuinely want to know their perspective and emotions around the situation. It gives them the space to express themselves honestly instead of just saying they're fine.

6. *Validate Before Offering Solutions*: When someone we love or care about is struggling, it's so instinctive to want to make

it better right away. But jumping to fix or solve things can accidentally invalidate how they feel. It's important to first acknowledge their emotions. For example, if your partner's stressed about a big project, instead of wanting to solve the problem right away, you can say, "I totally get why this is stressing you out. It seems overwhelming. I'm here for whatever you need. How can I support you?" Validating their feelings first and then asking how to help makes the person feel genuinely heard and cared for.

7. *Practice Emotional Intelligence*: Emotional intelligence is all about being aware of and in tune with emotions – both your own and others'. It's about understanding feelings, controlling your reactions, showing motivation and empathy, and having social awareness. Improving your emotional intelligence helps you get better at things like validating how people feel, expressing your own emotions constructively, and building stronger bonds. When you know how to identify and deal with feelings skillfully, you tend to handle interactions and relationships with more care, empathy, and nuance. For example, if a friend is upset about a conflict at work, someone with high emotional intelligence would listen patiently, express empathy for their feelings, and ask thoughtful questions to better understand their perspective. This provides the validation and support the friend needs. Developing emotional intelligence allows you to recognize emotions, respond thoughtfully, and deepen connections on a whole new level.

8. *Self-awareness and Reflection*: Developing self-awareness is the building block of emotional intelligence. It means tun-

ing into your own emotions and how they affect your mindset and behavior. Specifically, if you notice yourself feeling defensive or wanting to minimize someone's feelings, take a minute to reflect. Ask yourself - why am I reacting that way to this person opening up? What am I feeling right now? That self-understanding helps you respond with more empathy and care next time. When you're aware of your own emotional landscape, you can better understand and validate others. Self-awareness creates space to check in with your inner experience, so you can manage reactions skillfully and relate to people with openness. It lays the groundwork for emotional intelligence.

Keep in mind that the goal isn't always to agree with the other person's point of view - it's just about showing you accept their emotions as real and significant. Simple phrases that acknowledge their feelings go a long way. This simple act can have a profound impact on our relationships and our ability to connect with others. Implementing these kinds of empathetic habits in your interactions can create an environment where people feel safe to be open and heard.

Practice Scenario: Addressing Feelings of Neglect in a Relationship

Consider this scenario: Maria and Alex have been in a relationship for a few years. Lately, Maria has been feeling neglected. Alex has been busy with work and hasn't been spending as much time with her as he used to. Maria feels hurt and unimportant but is unsure how to express her feelings to Alex without causing a conflict.

One evening, Maria decides to talk to Alex. She says, "Alex, I've been feeling neglected lately. I understand that you're busy with work, but I miss spending time with you. I feel like we're drifting apart." Alex, surprised, responds, "But I'm doing all this work for us, Maria. I didn't realize you felt this way."

This is a common situation in many relationships where one partner might feel neglected or less prioritized due to the other partner's preoccupations. It's crucial in such situations to express feelings honestly and practice emotional validation.

Exercises and Reflection Points

Don't forget to utilize a notebook for jotting down your responses to these exercises, and maintain a journal for introspective contemplation on the situation.

Exercises:

1. Reflect on Maria's approach to expressing her feelings to Alex. Was it effective? Why or why not?

2. Imagine you are Alex. How would you respond to Maria's concerns in a way that validates her feelings? Write down what you would say.

3. Consider the steps to avoid invalidation discussed earlier in this chapter. How could they be applied in this scenario? Write down specific examples.

Reflection Points:

1. Reflect on a time when you were in Alex's position. How did you respond when someone expressed feelings of neglect or dissatisfaction to you? How could you have responded better?

2. Consider your immediate reaction when someone shares negative feelings or criticism with you. Do you tend to get defensive, dismissive, or try to validate their feelings? How can you work on improving your initial reactions?

3. Think about the role of active listening in this scenario. How might the situation have been different if Alex had been more attuned to Maria's feelings before she expressed them?

4. Reflect on the non-verbal cues you give when someone is expressing their feelings to you. Are they in line with the principles of validation? If not, what changes can you make?

5. How can you implement the practice of emotional validation in your daily interactions, not just in conflict situations but in regular conversations as well?

Remember, the goal of these exercises and reflection points is not to find a one-size-fits-all solution but to reflect on these situations and develop your understanding and practice of emotional validation.

My Notes

Chapter Three

Building Bridges, Not Walls

A s we continue our exploration of empathy and emotional validation, we now turn our attention to the practical applications of these concepts in our daily interactions. In this chapter, we will look at the subtle yet significant differences between reactive and responsive communication, the role of empathy and validation in mitigating conflicts, and practical steps to transform potential misunderstandings into mutual understanding. We will also provide practical exercises to facilitate bridge-building conversations and a real-life scenario to illustrate these concepts in action.

Let's begin with understanding the fine line between reactive and responsive communication.

Reactive vs. Responsive: The Fine Line in Communication

In our interactions with others, we often find ourselves either reacting or responding. These might sound alike, but they're actually two very different ways of communicating. And the approach we choose can really affect the health and quality of our relationships.

Reactive communication is driven by our immediate emotional responses. When we communicate reactively, our emotions take the lead, often resulting in interactions that are driven by fear, hurt feelings, or other intense emotions. If a colleague criticizes your work, your immediate reaction might be to defend yourself aggressively or withdraw from the conversation entirely. This type of communication can escalate conflicts and create barriers between individuals.

On the other hand, responsive communication involves a more thoughtful and deliberate approach. Responsive communicators take a moment to process their emotions, consider the other person's perspective, and choose their words carefully. They stand up for themselves assertively, not aggressively, and handle inter-actions with respect and diplomacy. For example, in response to the same criticism, a responsive communicator might take a deep breath, acknowledge the feedback, and ask for specific examples to understand better and improve.

The difference between reactive and responsive communication can be likened to the difference between a knee-jerk reflex and a deliberate action. While our reflexes are automatic and immediate, our actions are intentional and considered. Similarly, while reactive communication is automatic and emotion-driven, responsive communication is thoughtful and empathy-driven.

Understanding this distinction is the first step toward becoming a more effective communicator. By striving to be more responsive and less reactive, we can navigate our interactions with greater empathy, understanding, and respect, building bridges of connection rather than walls of misunderstanding.

In the following section, we will take a look at the role of empathy and validation in mitigating conflicts and nurturing mutual understanding.

The Role of Empathy and Validation in Mitigating Conflicts

Conflict is an inevitable part of human interaction. Whether it's a disagreement with a colleague at work, a misunderstanding with a friend, or a heated argument with a partner, conflicts can be challenging and emotionally draining. However, they also present opportunities for growth, understanding, and deeper connection, and this is where empathy and validation come into play.

Empathy, as we've discussed, is the ability to understand and share another person's feelings. It allows us to step into their shoes and see the situation from their perspective. In the context of conflict, empathy can help us understand the other person's viewpoint, even if we don't necessarily agree with it. This understanding can diffuse tension, prevent escalation, and open the door to resolution.

Picture this: two colleagues, Mark and David, have a disagreement about a project. Mark believes they should follow a specific strategy, whereas David believes they ought to adopt a different approach. Without empathy, this disagreement could quickly turn into a heated argument, jeopardizing their working relationship and possibly impacting the project's success.

However, if Mark makes an effort to empathize with David, he might realize that David's approach is based on his previous experiences with similar projects. This understanding doesn't mean Mark has to agree with David's approach, but it can help him communicate his viewpoint in a more understanding and respectful manner.

Validation, on the other hand, is the acknowledgment and acceptance of another person's feelings and experiences. In situations of conflict, validation can make the other person feel heard and understood, reducing defensiveness and encouraging open, honest communication.

Continuing with our example, if David feels that Mark is dismissing his ideas, he might become defensive, leading to further conflict. However, if Mark validates David's feelings - for example, by saying, "I understand why you believe this approach would work based on your past experiences" - David will likely feel heard and acknowledged. This validation can lower his defensiveness, making him more open to discussing the situation and finding a mutually agreeable solution.

Steps to Transform Potential Misunderstandings into Mutual Understanding

Misunderstandings are a common part of human interactions. They can lead to conflicts, strained relationships, and even emotional distress. However, with the right approach, we can transform these potential misunderstandings into mutual understanding. Here are some steps to help you navigate this process:

1. *Engage Fully in Conversations:* This is the first and most crucial step in avoiding misunderstandings. Engaging fully means giving your complete attention to the speaker, not allowing distractions to interrupt the flow of conversation, and responding in a way that shows you're genuinely absorbing what they're saying. It's not just about hearing the words; it's about understanding the emotions and intentions behind them.

2. *Clarify and Ask Questions:* If something is unclear, don't hesitate to ask for clarification. This can help prevent misunderstandings from escalating. As an illustration, if your colleague makes a statement that you find confusing, you could say, "I want to make sure I understand what you're saying. Are you suggesting that...?"

3. *Express Yourself Clearly and Concisely:* Be clear and direct in your communication. Avoid using ambiguous language that could lead to misunderstandings. If you're expressing a concern, for example, state the issue clearly and suggest a possible solution.

4. *Practice Empathy:* Try to understand the other person's perspective. This can help you respond in a way that acknowledges their feelings and experiences, which can lead to better understanding and less conflict.

5. *Be Patient and Open-Minded:* Misunderstandings can often be resolved with a bit of patience and open-mindedness. Be

willing to listen, understand, and consider the other person's point of view.

6. *Use "I" Statements:* Instead of starting your sentences with "you," which can come off as accusatory, start with "I." This can help you express your feelings without blaming or criticizing the other person. For example, instead of saying, "You never listen to me," you could say, "I feel unheard when I share my thoughts."

7. *Mind Your Non-Verbal Cues:* As I previously mentioned, your body language, facial expressions, and tone of voice can communicate a lot about your feelings and intentions. Make sure they align with your words and the message you want to convey. For example, maintaining eye contact and having an open posture can show you're receptive and interested in the conversation.

Practical Exercises to Foster Bridge-Building Conversations

As we make our way along the path to effective communication, it's essential to have practical tools that can help us apply the principles we've learned. This section provides a set of exercises designed to foster bridge-building conversations. These exercises are not just theoretical concepts but practical steps that you can incorporate into your daily interactions. They aim to enhance your understanding of empathy, validation, and the fine line between reactive and responsive communication.

As you engage in these exercises, remember that the goal is not perfection but progress. Let's explore these exercises in more detail.

Empathy Practice

This exercise involves consciously trying to put yourself in other people's shoes for some time; it can be an hour or an entire day, based on your emotional and mental capacity. This could be anyone from a colleague at work, a family member at home, or even a stranger you pass on the street. Try to understand their perspective, their feelings, and their motivations. This exercise is not about agreeing with their viewpoint but about understanding it. Reflect on how this exercise changes your interactions and responses. Did you find yourself being more patient, more understanding, or more compassionate? How did people respond to you when you approached them with empathy?

Active Listening Role-Play

This exercise requires a partner. You can pair up with a friend, a family member, or even a colleague. Take turns playing the role of the speaker and the listener. The listener should practice active listening techniques such as nodding, maintaining eye contact, and paraphrasing the speaker's words. The speaker can then provide feedback on how validated they felt during the conversation. This exercise can provide valuable insights into how your listening skills impact others and where you might need to improve.

Validation Journal

For this exercise, keep a journal for a week where you note down instances where you validated someone else's feelings or had your feelings validated. This could be in a conversation with a friend, during a meeting at work, or even while interacting with a sales-person at a store. Reflect on how these instances made you and the other person feel. Did you notice a change in the dynamic of the conversation when validation was present?

Non-Verbal Communication Practice

Spend some time in front of a mirror practicing your non-verbal cues. Pay attention to your facial expressions, body language, and gestures. Do they express empathy and comprehension? For example, try to keep a relaxed and open posture, sustain eye contact, and offer nods of agreement. Observe how these silent signals can transmit a sense of empathy and validation, even in the absence of spoken words.

Conflict Resolution Role-Play

This exercise involves role-playing a conflict scenario with a partner. It could be a disagreement about household chores, a misunder-standing at work, or any other conflict situation. Practice using empathetic and validating language to de-escalate the conflict and reach a mutual understanding. This exercise can help you under-stand how empathy and validation can transform conflicts into opportunities for deeper understanding and connection.

Mindful Communication

This exercise involves being mindful of your words before respond-ing to a conversation. While you are interacting with someone, it could be your partner or a friend, take a moment to consider whether your intended response is reactive or responsive. Is it likely to escalate or de-escalate the situation? Are you acknowledging the other person's feelings? Practice this mindful communication in your daily interactions and notice the impact it has on your conversations.

Remember, these exercises are not one-time act vities. They require continuous practice. The more you practice, the more natural these skills will become, and the more effectively you'll be able to develop bridge-building conversations.

Practice Scenario: An Argument About Shared Responsibilities in a Household

Meet Olivia and Brian, a couple who recently welcomed their first child, a beautiful baby boy named Ethan. Olivia is on maternity leave from her job as a nurse, and Brian works from home as a graphic designer. They're both thrilled to be new parents, but they're also navigating the challenges that come with this new phase of life.

One evening, after a long day of caring for Ethan, Olivia expressed her frustration to Brian. She felt overwhelmed with the constant cycle of feeding, changing, and soothing Ethan, on top of managing household chores. Olivia felt that Brian wasn't contributing enough to the household responsibilities, especially since he was working from home.

On the other hand, Brian felt he was doing his best. He was working full-time to provide for their family and also helping with Ethan whenever he could. He felt that Olivia didn't understand the pressures he was under at work.

This argument led to feelings of resentment and misunderstanding between Olivia and Brian. They both felt unheard and unappreciated, which only served to escalate the conflict.

Exercises and Reflection Points

Use a notebook to jot down your answers to these exercises and a journal to reflect on the situation. These exercises are designed to help you apply what you've learned about communication, empathy, and validation in real-life scenarios. As you reflect on Olivia and Brian's argument, consider how these principles could be applied in your own life to transform potential misunderstandings into mutual understanding.

Exercises:

1. Put Yourself in Their Shoes: Imagine you're Olivia. How would you feel in this situation? Now, imagine you're Brian. How would his feelings differ from Olivia's? Write down your thoughts in your notebook.

2. Identify the Issue: What is the main issue causing the argument between Olivia and Brian? Is it the unequal division of responsibilities, lack of communication, or something else? Write down the main issue and any underlying issues you can identify.

3. Propose a Solution: Based on what you've learned about effective communication and validation, propose a solution to Olivia and Brian's argument. How could they have approached this conversation differently? Write down your proposed solution in your notebook.

Reflection Points:

1. Consider the role of empathy in this scenario. How could empathy have changed the course of Olivia and Brian's argument?

2. Reflect on the importance of validation in resolving conflicts. How could validation have helped Olivia and Brian understand each other's perspectives?

3. Think about the difference between being reactive and responsive. How could Olivia and Brian have responded rather than reacted to each other's frustrations?

My Notes

Chapter Four

Navigating Personal Relationships

U nderstanding emotions in our personal relationships is more than just an important aspect of human interaction; it's a fundamental cornerstone. Emotions are the language of our inner experiences, shaping our connections with others. In this chapter, we discuss the dynamics of empathy in various relationships - friendships, family, and partnerships. We will explore practical techniques for validating feelings and fostering an environment where empathy thrives in our daily interactions. Additionally, we will examine the concept of empathy as a double-edged sword, illuminating both its benefits and potential challenges.

Through real-life scenarios and engaging exercises, this chapter aims to provide you with the tools and insights to navigate the emotional landscapes of your personal relationships more effectively.

The Dynamics of Empathy in Friendships, Family, and Partnerships

The dynamics of empathy in friendships, family, and partnerships are multifaceted and deeply impactful. Empathy, the ability to understand and share the feelings of others, is a fundamental component of our social interactions. It allows us to connect with others on a deeper level, resulting in stronger and more meaningful relationships.

In friendships, empathy plays a crucial role in establishing trust and mutual understanding. It allows us to be there for our friends in times of need, offering comfort and support. For instance, if your friend is going through a tough time at work, showing empathy would mean listening to his concerns, understanding his feelings, and offering support without judgment.

In family relationships, empathy helps to strengthen bonds and improve communication. It allows us to understand the perspectives of our family members, fostering a more harmonious and supportive family environment. For example, if your sister is upset about a disagreement with a friend, showing empathy would involve acknowledging her feelings, understanding her perspective, and offering comfort and advice if appropriate.

In partnerships or romantic relationships, empathy is key to maintaining a strong and healthy relationship. It allows us to understand our partner's feelings and needs, promoting mutual respect and understanding. If your partner is feeling stressed about a project at work, being empathetic would mean acknowledging their stress, understanding the challenges they're facing, and offering your support.

However, it's important to note that while empathy is a powerful tool for building solid relationships, it needs to be balanced with self-care. Constantly taking on the emotions of others can be emotionally draining, so it's fundamental to also take care of our own emotional needs.

In the following section, you will learn about valuable techniques to validate feelings in personal relationships. These techniques can help you improve your communication skills and develop healthier, more understanding relationships with those around you.

Techniques to Validate Feelings in Personal Relationships

As we've discussed, validating emotions is key for creating deep bonds in our close relationships - with friends, family, or romantic partners. Now let's go over some practical techniques you can use to help understand and validate people's feelings in your life. Putting these into practice can help strengthen empathy and connection.

1. *Show Genuine Curiosity:* When someone shares their feelings or experiences with you, it's important to show genuine curiosity. This means not just hearing their words but actively engaging with their emotions and experiences. For example, if your friend tells you about a challenging situation at work, you might ask, "What was the most difficult part of that situation for you?" This question demonstrates that you are not only curious but also invested in understanding their point of view. Try not to ask questions that might seem judgmental or dismissive, like "Why didn't you just ignore it?" or "Is it really that big of a deal?"

2. *Use Affirming Statements:* Affirming statements are a pow-

erful tool for validation. They communicate that you understand and acknowledge the other person's feelings. As a case in point, if your sister is expressing her anxiety about an upcoming exam, an affirming statement could be, "It's completely understandable that you're feeling anxious about your exam. Exams can be really stressful." Try not to make statements that might belittle her feelings, like "You always get good grades; why are you worried?" or "Just relax; it's just an exam."

3. *Offer Emotional Support:* Offering emotional support can be a simple yet effective way to validate someone's feelings. This could be as simple as saying, "I'm really sorry you're going through this. I'm here for you." This statement communicates that you're there for them, ready to provide support and comfort. Avoid responding in ways that might come off as indifferent or uncaring, like "Well, everyone goes through tough times" or "You'll get over it."

4. *Reflective Listening:* Reflective listening is a technique that involves repeating back or paraphrasing what the other person has said to ensure you've understood correctly. It shows that you're actively listening and trying to understand their perspective. For example, if your friend says, "I'm really upset because I feel like no one appreciates my work," you might respond, "So, you feel that your efforts aren't being recognized and you're feeling unappreciated at work. That must be really hard." Stay away from responses that could distort their message or make assumptions, like "So, you're upset because you want a promotion?" or "You're just being too sensitive."

5. *Normalize Their Feelings:* Normalizing someone's feelings means acknowledging that their emotions are valid and understandable given their situation. You might say something like, "Anyone in your situation would feel stressed. It's completely normal." Sentences like "Why are you so stressed? It's not a big deal" or "You're the only one who reacts like this" might make them feel abnormal or overreactive and, in some cases, can severely harm the relationship or friendship.

6. *Practice Patience:* Validation requires patience. It takes time to fully understand someone else's perspective and to communicate that understanding effectively. If your partner is upset about something, take the time to listen to their feelings without rushing to offer solutions or advice. Steer clear of responses that might appear impatient or dismissive, like "Can we talk about this later?" or "Just get over it."

7. *Use Body Language:* Non-verbal cues can also convey validation. Maintaining eye contact, nodding your head, and having an open body posture can all signal to the other person that you are engaged and empathetic. Such as, if your friend is sharing a difficult experience, leaning in, maintaining eye contact, and nodding can show that you're fully present and attentive. Avoid body language that might seem disinterested or dismissive, like looking at your phone, crossing your arms, or looking away frequently.

8. *Avoid Minimizing Language:* Minimizing someone's feelings can be very invalidating. Phrases like "It's not a big deal" or "You're overreacting" can make the other person feel like their feelings are not important or valid. Instead,

acknowledge the significance of their feelings with statements like, "That sounds really tough" or "Your feelings are important." Refrain from responses that might belittle their feelings or their situation, like "There are people who have it worse" or "You're making a mountain out of a molehill."

Incorporating these methods into your personal bonds can foster a climate where understanding and respect are reciprocal. These approaches will guide you in handling emotionally charged discussions with sensitivity and affirmation, thereby enhancing your relationships with others. In the next section, we'll explore how to create an empathetic space in daily personal interactions.

Creating an Empathetic Space in Daily Personal Interactions

Creating an empathetic space in our daily human encounters involves establishing an environment in which empathy is the norm, in which everyone feels heard, understood, and valued. It's not just about understanding and validating the feelings of others but also about how we consistently practice empathy in our everyday interactions.

Empathy is not a one-time act. It's a habit that needs to be cultivated and practiced consistently. This means showing empathy not just when someone is visibly upset but also in everyday situations. For example, if your colleague seems quieter than usual, you might ask them how they're doing, showing that you notice and care about their well-being.

In addition to this, open and honest communication is a cornerstone of an empathetic space. This involves creating an environment where people feel safe expressing their thoughts and feelings without fear of judgment or dismissal. In a family setting, this could mean having regular family meetings where everyone is encouraged to share their feelings and concerns.

Active listening is another crucial part of creating an empathetic space. It's not just about hearing the words that another person is saying but also understanding and reflecting on the emotions behind those words. If your friend is talking about a problem, active listening would mean not only understanding the details of the problem but also recognizing and acknowledging any stress or frustration they may be experiencing.

Moreover, an empathetic space is one where everyone's emotional boundaries are respected. This means understanding and respecting when someone needs space and not pushing them to share more than they're comfortable with. If a friend says they don't want to talk about a certain topic, respecting their boundary means not pressing them further on that topic.

Maintaining a non-judgmental attitude is essential for cultivating empathy. This means acknowledging and respecting the emotions of others, even if they don't align with your views or experiences. To illustrate, if your partner is upset about something that seems trivial to you, a non-judgmental attitude would involve validating their feelings rather than dismissing them.

Lastly, being emotionally available to others is a key part of creating an empathetic space. This means being willing to share your own feelings and experiences, as well as being open to the feelings and experiences of others. For example, if a family member is going through a difficult time, being emotionally available might mean sharing your own experiences with similar difficulties to help them feel less alone.

Empathy: A Double-Edged Sword

While empathy is the golden thread in meaningful communication and bonds, it can sometimes tangle in unexpected ways and turn into a double-edged sword. But what does it mean? On one side, empathy allows us to connect with others on a profound level. It enables us to understand their feelings, perspectives, and experiences, building a sense of closeness and mutual understanding. This connection can be incredibly enriching, leading to more robust, meaningful relationships.

For instance, when a friend is going through a tough time, our empathetic response allows us to understand their pain, providing comfort and support. It's this empathetic connection that can make them feel less alone in their struggles, knowing that someone else understands what they're going through.

However, the other edge of the sword reveals potential challenges associated with empathy. At times, our empathetic nature can lead us to absorb the emotions of others, especially when they are suppressing or denying their feelings. This phenomenon, often unconscious, can result in us experiencing emotions that are not our own. In psychoanalysis, it is called "projective identification," where one person unconsciously projects their unacknowledged feelings onto another person, who then experiences those feelings. This can often occur in close relationships, where one person becomes a 'screen' for the other's projections.

Let me make an example; consider a scenario where you spend time with a friend who, on the surface, appears cheerful. However, they're actually suppressing feelings of sadness. Unknowingly, you might find yourself feeling a wave of sadness after your interaction. This can be confusing and emotionally draining, especially if you're not aware of what's happening.

Furthermore, there can be instances where individuals unconsciously prefer others to feel their feelings for them. This can create an imbalance in the relationship, leading to emotional exhaustion for the person who is constantly feeling the other's emotions. This is particularly common in close relationships where emotional boundaries may not be as defined but are fundamental for our mental health. In fact, this is where setting boundaries comes in.

Establishing boundaries is a critical component in managing the dual nature of empathy which is often overlooked and remains ambiguous for many. Setting boundaries helps ensure being empathic connects you to others instead of wiping you out emotionally or stressing you out. In other words, boundaries allow empathy to bring you closer together, not drain you.

But what do we mean when we talk about boundaries? Boundaries, in this context, refer to the emotional limits that we set with others. They help us distinguish our own feelings and needs from those of others. This is particularly important when we're empathetic, as we can easily absorb the emotions of those around us. Without clear boundaries, we risk losing ourselves in the feelings of others, which can lead to emotional exhaustion and a loss of our own emotional clarity.

Let's say that you have a friend who often comes to you with their problems. You're naturally empathetic, so you listen and offer support. However, you find that after these interactions, you're left feeling drained and overwhelmed or even stressed or anxious. This is where setting boundaries comes in.

Setting boundaries can be as simple as taking time for self-care after emotionally intense interactions. This could involve activities that help you recharge and reconnect with your own feelings, such as meditation, journaling, or simply spending some quiet time alone. These practices can help you to 'reset' emotionally, allowing you to distinguish your own feelings from those you've absorbed from others.

Another important aspect of setting boundaries is learning to say 'no.' This can be particularly challenging for empathetic people, as they naturally want to help and support others. However, constantly prioritizing the needs of others over our own can lead to burnout. For example, if your friend calls you late at night wanting to talk about their issues with their new partner, and you have an early morning meeting the next day, it's absolutely okay to tell them that you can't talk at that moment and you need to practice prioritizing and protecting yourself. It's important to remember that saying 'no' to others can sometimes mean saying 'yes' to ourselves. It's not only okay to prioritize your own needs, but it's necessary for your emotional wellbeing.

Communicating your boundaries to others is also crucial. This might involve having open and honest conversations about your emotional needs and limits with the people in your life. Should you discover that certain subjects take an emotional toll on you, it's perfectly acceptable to inform others and request that they honor your boundaries.

If a close friend frequently vents to you about their ongoing issues with their mom, it's perfectly acceptable to express your need for balance. You might say, "I value our friendship, and I want to be there for you and support you, but the intensity of these conversations can be overwhelming for me. I also need to take care of my own emotional wellbeing. Can we find a balance that works for both of us?"

Or you find that you're often feeling emotionally drained after interactions with a particular person, it might be helpful to have a conversation with them about it. This doesn't mean blaming them for your feelings but rather expressing your experience and exploring ways to create a more balanced emotional dynamic.

In fact, it's essential to engage in such honest, respectful discussions with those around you about your emotional boundaries and requirements; it benefits you and the relationship.

By setting clear emotional boundaries, we can ensure that our empathy serves as a powerful tool for connection and understanding rather than leading to emotional exhaustion or confusion. This allows us to maintain healthy, balanced relationships where empathy enhances our connections rather than draining our emotional resources.

Practice Scenario: Reconnecting with a Distant Family Member

Imagine this situation: After many years of minimal contact, you decide to reconnect with your older brother. The distance between you two grew over the years due to a misunderstanding that happened during your teenage years. You both have grown and changed since then, and you feel it's time to bridge the gap.

Here's how you might approach this:

1. *Initial Contact:* You decide to reach out to your brother with a simple, non-confrontational message. You might say something like, "Hi, it's been a while since we last talked. I've been thinking about our relationship, and I would like to reconnect if you're open to it."

2. *Expressing Your Intentions:* In your next conversation, you express your intentions clearly. You might say, "I've realized how much I miss having you in my life. I know we had our differences in the past, but I believe we've both grown since then. I would like for us to try and rebuild our relationship."

3. *Listening and Validating:* As your brother shares his feelings about the past and the present, you listen attentively and validate his feelings. You might say, "I understand why you felt hurt, and I'm sorry for my part in that. Your feelings are valid, and I appreciate you sharing them with me."

4. *Sharing Your Feelings:* You also take the opportunity to share your feelings and experiences. You might say, "I also felt hurt when we drifted apart. But I believe we can learn from our

past and build a stronger relationship moving forward."

5. *Setting Boundaries:* As you reconnect, you both discuss and set boundaries to ensure a healthy relationship. You might say, "I think it's important for us to respect each other's space and feelings as we reconnect. Let's agree to communicate openly and honestly about our needs and boundaries."

Exercises and Reflection Points

I have prepared a set of exercises and reflection points for you. These are designed to help you apply the concepts we've discussed in real-life scenarios. They will encourage you to think deeply about your relationships, feelings, and communication patterns. Remember to use a notebook to write down your thoughts, feelings, and reflections during these exercises. It's a great way to track your progress and contemplate your journey.

Exercises:

1. Think about a relationship in your life that you'd like to reconnect. Write down what caused the distance and what has changed since then.

2. Write a draft of the initial message you would send to this person. Remember to keep it simple, non-confrontational, and open-ended.

3. Practice active listening and validation with a friend or family member. Notice how it impacts the conversation and the other person's openness.

4. Write a letter to the person you want to reconnect with. In this letter, express your feelings, your intentions, and your hopes for the future of your relationship. Keep in mind that you don't have to send this letter; it's just an exercise to help you clarify your thoughts and feelings.

Reflection Points:

1. Consider the potential responses you might receive. How would you react if the response is positive? What about if it's negative or non-committal?

2. Reflect on your own boundaries. What do you need in your relationships to feel respected and comfortable? How can you communicate these boundaries effectively?

3. Reflection Point: As you contemplate reconnecting with a distant family member, consider the role empathy plays in this process. How does understanding their feelings and perspective influence your approach? Reflect on the balance between empathy and maintaining your own emotional well-being in this situation.

My Notes

Chapter Five

Emotional Validation in Professional Landscapes

I n the workplace, empathy is a powerful tool for bringing people together and driving success. Empathy in professional settings is about truly seeking to understand colleagues' perspectives, validating their emotions or concerns, and responding in ways that make them feel genuinely heard and valued. When team members feel their feelings are acknowledged, it catalyzes more open communication, stronger collaboration, and more inspiring leadership. By learning to validate emotions effectively, we can transform disconnected teams into cohesive units focused on shared goals.

Furthermore, empathy can inspire innovative thinking. Leaders who demonstrate empathy motivate their team members to generate new ideas and solutions. By considering the perspectives of others, we can better address the needs and expectations of our target audience or clients.

But empathy in professional settings goes beyond interpersonal relationships. It's also about creating an environment that respects and values the emotional well-being of all members. This includes recognizing the signs of burnout, addressing conflicts in a constructive manner, and promoting a culture of emotional intelligence.

In this chapter, we'll look into the application of validation across several professional settings, including therapy, counseling, leadership, and customer relations. You'll discover strategies to develop an environment anchored in mutual respect and understanding. Additionally, I will present real-world scenarios highlighting emotional validation in the workplace. This will include topics such as resolving team conflicts, guiding feedback sessions, managing customer complaints, facilitating team brainstorming sessions, and tackling employee burnout.

Applying Validation in Therapy, Counseling, Leadership, and Customer Relations

As you may have gathered, validation is a cornerstone of building rapport, trust, and understanding not only in interpersonal relationships but also in many professional contexts. Actually, effectively validating emotions is key to cultivating strong, healthy relationships, whether in a therapeutic setting, a leadership role, or customer-facing services. In this section, you will discover practical techniques for applying validation across diverse professional landscapes.

Validation in Therapy

In the realm of therapy, validation plays a pivotal role. It's a fundamental part of the therapeutic process, a technique that therapists employ to build a sense of security and trust with their clients. When a therapist validates their client's feelings and experiences, they are essentially communicating, "I hear you. I see you. Your feelings are real, and they matter." This can be a potent message, one that helps the client feel understood and accepted, which is vital for the therapeutic relationship to work.

Consider a client who is wrestling with feelings of guilt and shame over a past mistake. They might be struggling to forgive themselves, caught in a cycle of self-blame and regret. In this situation, a therapist might validate these feelings by saying something like, "It's understandable that you're feeling this way. This situation has clearly had a profound impact on you." This validation doesn't mean the therapist is agreeing with the client's self-blame but rather acknowledging the pain and struggle the client is experiencing.

This validation can encourage the client to open up further to explore their feelings and experiences more deeply. It can create a space for them to understand their guilt and shame better and ultimately start the healing process.

But validation in therapy extends beyond just acknowledging feelings. It's also about affirming the client's strengths, resilience, and efforts. A therapist might validate a client's coping strategies by saying, "I can see how hard you're working to deal with this. It takes a lot of courage to face these difficult feelings." This can help the client recognize their own strength and resilience, which can be really empowering.

Therapists can use validation in several ways to enhance the therapeutic process and build stronger bonds with their clients. Here are a few examples:

1. *Acknowledging Emotions:* A therapist can validate a client's feelings by acknowledging them and expressing understanding. For example, a therapist might say, "It sounds like you're feeling really overwhelmed right now. That's a completely understandable response to what you're going through."

2. *Reflecting Feelings:* Therapists can reflect the client's feelings back to them, which can help the client feel heard and understood. For example, if a client is expressing frustration, the therapist might say, "I can hear the frustration in your voice. It's clear that this situation is really challenging for you."

3. *Normalizing Emotions:* Therapists can validate clients' emotions by normalizing them. This can help clients feel that their reactions are normal and expected, given their circumstances. A therapist might say, "Anyone in your situation would likely feel the same way. It's normal to feel anxious when facing such a big change."

4. *Expressing Empathy:* Therapists can validate clients' experiences by expressing empathy. This involves not only understanding the client's feelings but also communicating that understanding in a compassionate way. For example, a therapist might say, "I can only imagine how difficult this must be for you. It's clear that you're doing your best in a really tough situation."

5. *Validating Efforts and Progress:* Therapists can validate clients' efforts and progress, which can help boost their self-esteem and motivation. Namely, a therapist might say,

"I've noticed how hard you've been working on your coping strategies. I'm so impressed by the progress you've made. "

6. *Using Non-Verbal Validation:* Therapists can also use non-verbal cues to validate their clients' feelings. This could be nodding in understanding, maintaining eye contact, or using open body language to convey acceptance and un-derstanding.

In essence, validation in therapy is about creating a safe, accepting space where clients can explore their feelings and experiences with-out fear of judgment or rejection. It's about helping clients feel seen and heard and, ultimately, helping them heal. It's a powerful tool for therapists to facilitate personal growth and emotional healing.

Validation in Counseling

In the counseling setting, validation plays a unique role. While therapy often involves a deep exploration of past experiences and underlying psychological patterns, counseling tends to focus more on the present and future, providing practical advice and strategies to help clients navigate their current challenges.

In this context, validation is used as a tool to acknowledge and affirm the client's feelings and experiences, building a sense of trust and rapport. This can be particularly important in counseling, where the focus is often on helping clients to develop new skills and strategies to manage their emotions and relationships.

Here are some ways a counselor can apply validation:

1. *Active Listening:* Active listening is a key skill in counseling.

It is about entirely focusing on the client, avoiding distractions, and responding in a way that shows understanding and respect for their feelings. This can be as simple as nodding in agreement, maintaining eye contact, or using verbal cues like "I see" or "I understand."

2. *Reflecting Feelings:* This involves identifying and articulating the emotions that the client is expressing, even if they haven't explicitly named them. For example, if a client is talking about a stressful situation at work, the counselor might say, "It sounds like that situation is causing you a lot of stress and frustration."

3. *Affirming Strengths:* In counseling, it's crucial to not only acknowledge the client's struggles but also to affirm their strengths and capabilities. This can help to boost their self-esteem and resilience. For example, the counselor might say, "I can see that you're really committed to improving this situation, and that takes a lot of courage."

4. *Normalizing Experiences:* Sometimes, clients may feel isolated or abnormal because of their feelings or experiences. In these cases, the counselor can use validation to normalize these experiences, reassuring the client that it's okay to feel the way they do. For example, the counselor might say, "Many people feel overwhelmed in situations like this. It's a normal reaction."

5. *Expressing Empathy:* This involves showing genuine understanding and compassion for the client's experiences. This can help the client to feel seen and understood, fostering a sense of connection and trust. For example, the counselor

might say, "That sounds really tough. I can imagine how hard it must be for you."

Validation in Leadership

In the context of leadership, the application of validation takes on a unique and critical role. Leaders are in a position where their words and actions can significantly impact the people they lead. By validating their team members, leaders can foster a sense of trust, respect, and mutual understanding, which are fundamental to a healthy and productive work environment.

Let's consider a leader in a corporate setting. This leader is responsible for a diverse team, each member with their own unique experiences, viewpoints, and emotions. The leader's role is not just to manage tasks and deadlines but also to navigate the complex web of interpersonal relationships within the team. Here, the power of validation becomes evident.

When a team member shares an idea during a meeting, the leader can validate this contribution by acknowledging the thought and effort that went into it. This doesn't necessarily mean agreeing with the idea but rather recognizing the value of the team member's input. This can be as simple as saying, "I appreciate your perspective on this. It's clear you've put a lot of thought into it."

Similarly, when a team member expresses frustration or concern, the leader can validate these feelings. Instead of dismissing the problem or immediately jumping to problem-solving, the leader can first acknowledge the team member's feelings. Case in point, the leader might say, "I can see why this situation is frustrating for you. Your feelings are completely understandable."

In both of these examples, the leader is using validation to create an environment where team members feel heard, understood, and valued. Doing this not only improves the individuals' sense of self-worth but also builds a sense of trust and mutual respect within the team. When team members feel their perspectives are validated, it creates an environment where people are more open and willing to work together.

However, it's important to note that validation in leadership is about crafting a culture where empathy, respect, and understanding are the norm. It means genuinely valuing the distinct insights every team member offers. And at its core, it's about leading with realness, heartfelt compassion, and unwavering respect.

Validation in Customer Relations

In the sphere of customer relations, the role of validation is paramount. It extends beyond the mere provision of a product or service, reaching into the realm of recognizing and empathizing with the customer's needs, emotions, and experiences. This empathetic understanding builds a solid basis for lasting customer relationships, nurturing higher satisfaction, loyalty, and even positive word-of-mouth.

When we talk about validation in the context of customer relations, we refer to acknowledging and affirming the customer's emotions and experiences. This could be as straightforward as recognizing a customer's disappointment with a product malfunction or as intricate as comprehending a customer's unique needs and preferences.

For example, consider a customer expressing frustration over a product defect. A customer service representative could respond, "I can see why this situation would upset you. Dealing with a product malfunction can indeed be frustrating. Let's work together to find a solution." This response not only acknowledges the customer's emotions but also conveys that the representative is on their side, ready to assist and support.

On a larger scale, validation can also mean understanding what your overall customer base wants and needs. You can do surveys to learn what customers like about your products and use that information to improve. For example, if surveys show that your customers are looking for eco-friendly options, you could consider making production more sustainable.

In each of these situations, validation enhances your customer relationships, paving the way for increased satisfaction, loyalty, and business success in the long run. It's about more than just closing a sale; it's about cultivating a relationship rooted in understanding, respect, and mutual benefit.

Now, let's explore some additional methods that can be employed in customer relations:

1. *Proactive Communication:* Keep the customer informed about the progress of their issue. This shows that you value their time and are actively working on their concern.

2. *Empathy in Action:* Show understanding not just in words but also in actions. If a product is faulty, offer a replacement or refund. If a service is delayed, provide an estimated time of resolution.

3. *Training and Development:* Equip your customer service team with the skills to handle difficult situations and emo-

tionally charged customers. Regular training sessions can help them understand the importance of empathy and validation in customer interactions.

4. *Feedback Loop:* Encourage customers to provide feedback on their experience. This not only gives them a voice but also helps you identify areas of improvement.

Fostering a Professional Environment Rooted in Mutual Respect and Understanding

Creating a professional environment that is rooted in mutual respect and understanding is a shared responsibility. While leaders play a crucial role in setting the tone, every individual within the organization contributes to the overall culture. Here are some strategies that can be employed by both leaders and employees:

Model Respectful Behavior

Modeling respectful behavior is about embodying the values and behaviors you wish to see in your workplace. It's about demonstrating through your actions how to interact with others in a respectful and considerate manner. This applies to everyone in the workplace, from leaders to employees.

As a leader, your actions set the tone for the entire team or organization. Your team members will observe how you behave and often mirror those behaviors. If you consistently treat everyone with kindness and respect, regardless of their role or status, your team members are likely to do the same. If you handle conflicts calmly and constructively, your team will learn to do the same when they face conflicts.

Consider a situation where a project doesn't go as planned. Instead of placing blame, you might say, "I understand that we're all disappointed with how this project turned out. Let's discuss what we can learn from this and how we can improve for next time." This shows your team that you value learning and growth over blame and criticism.

As an employee, your actions also have an impact. Your peers will notice how you behave and may follow your example. If you consistently show respect for others' ideas during team meetings, even when you disagree, others may start to do the same. If you make an effort to acknowledge your colleagues' hard work and contributions, they will feel valued and appreciated.

Imagine a situation where a colleague shares an idea that you disagree with. Instead of dismissing it outright, you might say, "I see where you're coming from, but I have a different perspective. Can we discuss this further?" This shows that you respect their ideas, even when you disagree.

Modeling respectful behavior also extends to how you treat people outside of your immediate team or organization. If you're in a customer-facing role, treating customers with respect and understanding can not only improve customer satisfaction but also set a positive example for your peers.

In all these ways, modeling respectful behavior can help create a professional environment rooted in mutual respect and understanding. It's about showing through your actions what it means to treat others with respect and inspire others to do the same.

Communicate Openly and Honestly

Open and honest communication is the cornerstone of a respectful and understanding professional environment. It's about sharing your thoughts, feelings, and ideas in a respectful, constructive way and also being receptive to the perspectives of others. It's about creating a space where everyone feels heard and valued.

Suppose you're an employee who's feeling overwhelmed by your workload. Instead of keeping these feelings to yourself or venting to your coworkers, you decide to have a conversation with your manager. You might say, "I've been feeling overwhelmed with my current workload. I'm committed to doing my best work, but I'm worried that the volume of tasks might impact the quality of my output. Could we discuss possible solutions?"

In this situation, you're not only expressing your feelings and concerns, but you're also showing a willingness to find solutions. You're demonstrating respect for your manager by addressing the issue directly with them rather than discussing it behind their back. This open and honest communication can lead to a better understanding of each other's perspectives and needs and can help to cultivate a more supportive and understanding work environment.

Likewise, if you're a leader, open and honest communication involves not only sharing your own thoughts and expectations but also being open to feedback from your team. It's about creating a space where your team members feel comfortable expressing their ideas, concerns, and suggestions.

During team meetings, you might encourage your team members to share their ideas and feedback. You might say, "I value all of your perspectives, and I'm interested in hearing your ideas on how we can improve our workflow. Please feel free to share your thoughts."

This encourages open communication and shows your team that you value their input and are open to new ideas.

Value Diversity

Recognizing and appreciating diversity is a powerful strategy to cultivate a professional environment that thrives on mutual respect and understanding. Every team member brings a unique blend of skills, experiences, and perspectives that can greatly enrich the collective output. By valuing this diversity, we can promote an inclusive work environment that not only respects individual differences but also leverages them for innovation and problem-solving.

Consider a scenario where you're part of a project team. Each team member comes from a different background, has different skills, and sees the world through a unique lens. When respected and valued, these differences can be a tremendous asset to the team.

For example, a team member with a background in design might approach a problem differently than someone with a background in engineering. The designer might focus on the user experience and aesthetics, while the engineer might focus on functionality and efficiency. Both perspectives are valid, valuable and can complement each other to create a more well-rounded solution.

As a team leader or a team member, you can nurture this diversity by encouraging each team member to share their unique ideas and viewpoints. You might facilitate a brainstorming session where each team member is invited to contribute their ideas. You could say, "We all have different skills and perspectives, and that's what makes our team strong. Let's all share our ideas and see what creative solutions we can come up with together."

By valuing diversity, you not only establish a more inclusive and respectful workplace but also promote innovation and creativity. You're sending a message that every team member's input is valued, and their unique perspective can contribute to the team's success. This can lead to higher levels of team engagement, creativity, and productivity and, ultimately, a more successful project outcome.

Provide and Receive Feedback Constructively

Constructive feedback is a cornerstone of professional growth and development. It's a two-way street that involves both giving and receiving feedback in a manner that promotes understanding, respect, and improvement. The key is to focus on the behavior or performance, not the person, and to approach the conversation with an open mind and a willingness to learn.

Let's consider two cases - one as a leader and one as an employee:

Case #1: As a Leader Imagine you're a team leader, and one of your team members has been consistently late for meetings. Instead of making a blanket statement like "You're always late," which can come off as accusatory and personal, you might approach the situation more constructively. You could say, "I've noticed that you've been late to our last few meetings. I understand that unexpected things can come up. Is there something that's been preventing you from arriving on time?" This approach focuses on the behavior (being late) rather than the person and opens up a dialogue where the team member can share their perspective or any challenges they're facing.

Case #2: As an Employee Now, let's say you're an employee, and your manager has given you feedback that your reports have been lacking in detail. Instead of taking this feedback as a personal attack, see it as an opportunity for growth. You might respond by saying, "Thank you for your feedback. I understand the importance of detailed reports in our decision-making process. Can you provide some specific examples where more detail would have been beneficial? This will help me understand better and improve my future reports." This response shows that you're open to feedback and are proactive about using it to improve your performance.

In both scenarios, the focus is on the behavior or performance, not the person. The feedback is delivered and received in a respectful and constructive way, helping to promote an environment of mutual respect and understanding. By approaching feedback in this way, we can promote personal and professional growth, improve performance, and build stronger, more effective teams.

Participate in Team Building

The act of participating in team-building activities is a powerful strategy to fortify relationships, enhance communication, and cultivate mutual respect within a professional environment. These activities, whether they are structured or informal, provide shared experiences that can significantly contribute to a sense of unity and mutual understanding among team members.

Think about the effect of a professional development workshop. In this collaborative setting, coworkers learn and grow their abilities together. For example, a workshop on conflict resolution provides practical techniques for handling disputes constructively. With the whole team acquiring these shared strategies, it establishes common ground for managing conflicts respectfully.

On the other hand, informal social events, such as team lunches or outings, offer a relaxed environment for team members to connect on a more personal level. For example, a team outing to a local escape room or a group cooking class allows team members to interact outside the usual work context. These activities provide opportunities to appreciate each other's unique skills and personalities, leading to stronger personal connections and a deeper sense of mutual esteem.

Furthermore, team-building activities can serve as a platform for open communication and conflict resolution. When team members collaborate towards a common goal, they gain a better understanding of each other's perspectives and work styles. This understanding can lead to more effective conflict resolution, improved communication, and a more harmonious work environment.

Support Policies that Promote Respect

One of the key strategies to build a professional environment rooted in mutual respect and understanding is to support and adhere to workplace policies that promote respectful behavior. These policies set the standard for how individuals should interact with each other in the workplace, and they play a crucial role in creating a respectful and inclusive environment.

In particular, consider the impact of a comprehensive anti-discrimination policy. This policy sends a clear message that all forms of discrimination, whether based on race, gender, age, religion, or any other characteristic, are not tolerated. By adhering to this policy and taking action when you see violations, you contribute to a culture of respect and equality.

In addition, if you notice that certain essential policies are missing in your workplace, don't hesitate to advocate for them. For
example, if your workplace lacks a clear policy on preventing
and addressing harassment, it's important to bring this to the attention of your human resources department or your supervisor.
You could highlight the importance of such a policy in creating
a safe and respectful work environment and offer to be part of a
committee to help develop it.

In the same vein, if your workplace doesn't have a policy that
recognizes and accommodates the needs of employees with dis-
abilities, advocating for creating such a policy can help ensure
that all employees are treated with respect and understanding.

When you actively support and adhere to respectful policies, you
create a culture of inclusion where respect becomes a daily reality
rather than an abstract concept. Your example also inspires others
to follow suit in the workplace.

Practical Scenarios of Emotional Validation in the Workplace

In this section, we will explore various practical scenarios where
emotional validation can be applied in the workplace. You
will reflect and learn how to resolve team conflicts, conduct
feedback sessions, handle customer complaints, facilitate team
brainstorming, and address employee burnout through the lens
of emotional validation.

#1 – Resolving team conflicts: Validating each member's perspective to find common ground

Imagine you're a team leader, and there's a conflict brewing within your team. Two team members, let's call them Liam and Taylor, have a disagreement about the direction of a project. Liam believes that the team should focus on feature A, while Taylor insists that feature B is more important. The disagreement has escalated, and it's starting to affect the team's productivity.

As a leader, your role is to mediate the conflict and guide your team toward a resolution. Here's where emotional validation comes into play:

1. *Acknowledge each person's perspective:* Start by acknowledging each team member's viewpoint. You might say, "Liam, I understand that you believe feature A is crucial for our project. You've raised some valid points about its potential benefits." Then, do the same for Taylor. This shows that you're listening to both sides and that you value their input.

2. *Validate their feelings:* Next, to validate their feelings, you could say, "I can see why this disagreement is causing tension. It's clear that both of you are passionate about the project and want what's best for it. Your feelings are completely understandable."

3. *Encourage open communication:* Encourage Liam and Taylor to express their thoughts and feelings about the situation. Facilitate a conversation where they can discuss their viewpoints openly and honestly. This can help them understand each other's perspectives better.

4. *Guide towards a solution:* Once everyone's feelings and perspectives have been acknowledged and validated, guide the team towards a solution. This might involve finding a compromise, seeking input from the rest of the team, or making a decision based on the project's priorities and constraints.

Fostering a more cooperative and respectful team environment is possible when you help defuse conflict by validating the perspectives and feelings of each team member.

#2 – Feedback Sessions – Using Validation to Convey Constructive Criticism and Acknowledging Efforts

Imagine you're a team leader, and it's time for the quarterly feedback sessions. One of your team members, let's call him James, has been struggling with meeting deadlines. You've noticed that while James's work is of high quality, his time management skills need improvement. Here's how you might use validation in this feedback session:

1. *Start by acknowledging James's efforts:* "James, I want to start by saying that the quality of your work is impressive. Your attention to detail and dedication are evident in the projects you've completed."

2. *Next, convey your constructive criticism using validation:* "I've noticed that you've had some difficulty meeting deadlines. I understand that you put a lot of effort into your work and want to produce the best results possible, which can take time."

3. *Then, validate his feelings about the situation:* "It must be

stressful to feel like you're always racing against the clock. I can see how that could be overwhelming."

4. *Offer support and discuss solutions:* "I want to support you in finding ways to manage your time more effectively. Perhaps we can look at prioritizing tasks differently or finding tools that can help you track your progress."

5. *End the session by validating his ability to improve*: "I have confidence in your ability to overcome this challenge. You've shown great adaptability in the past, and I believe you can do it again."

In this scenario, you've not only provided James with constructive feedback but also validated his efforts and feelings. This approach can make the feedback session a more positive experience for James and increase the likelihood of him taking the feedback onboard and making the necessary changes.

#3 – Handling customer complaints: Validating Customer Experiences to Enhance Trust and Loyalty

Let's imagine Lucas, a customer service representative, is dealing with a customer complaint. Claire, a long-time customer, has called to express her dissatisfaction with a recent product she purchased.

Claire explains that the product she purchased was not functioning as advertised. She's frustrated because she had high expectations based on her previous positive experiences with the company's products.

Here's how Lucas might use validation to handle this situation:

1. *Listen and Acknowledge:* Lucas starts by listening to Claire's complaint without interrupting. He lets her express her frustration and disappointment. Once she's finished, he acknowledges her feelings by saying, "I understand why you're upset, Claire. It's not what you expect from our products, and for that, I'm truly sorry."

2. *Validate the Customer's Experience:* Lucas then validates Claire's experience. He might say, "It sounds like you've had a really disappointing experience, Claire. I can see why you'd be upset if the product didn't meet your expectations. You've trusted us with your business, and it seems like we've let you down this time."

3. *Offer Assistance:* Lucas then offers to help resolve the issue. He might say, "I'm here to help, Claire. Let's see what we can do to make this right for you. Would a replacement product or a refund be a suitable solution for you?"

4. *Follow Through:* Lucas ensures to follow through on his promises. If he promises to escalate an issue to a higher department, he acts on it without delay. He can say, "I've forwarded your complaint to our product team, Claire. They're looking into it, and we'll get back to you as soon as we have more information."

5. *Check-In:* After the issue has been resolved, Lucas checks in with Claire to ensure she's satisfied with the solution. He could say, "I wanted to check in and see how things are going with the replacement product, Claire. Is everything working as expected now?"

Throughout the conversation, Lucas maintains a calm and empathetic tone. He doesn't get defensive or try to minimize Claire's feelings. Instead, he validates her experience and works to find a solution. By using validation in this way, Lucas is helping to resolve Claire's immediate complaint and building a stronger relationship with her. He's showing Claire that her feelings and experiences are valid, which can lead to increased customer satisfaction and loyalty.

#4 – Facilitating Team Brainstorming: Validating Ideas to Foster Creativity and Inclusiveness

Let's say you are a team leader in a tech company, and you're tasked with facilitating a brainstorming session to come up with innovative ideas for a new project.

The team is diverse, with members from different departments with unique perspectives and expertise. As the facilitator, your role is to create an environment where everyone feels comfortable sharing their ideas and all ideas are validated and considered.

You start the session by setting the stage. You explain the purpose of the brainstorming session, the project at hand, and what you hope to achieve by the end of the session. You also emphasize the importance of every team member's contribution and encourage them to share their ideas freely.

As the ideas start flowing, you make sure to validate each one. For example, when Noah, a software engineer, suggests a technical feature that could enhance the project, you might say, "That's an interesting idea, Noah. The technical enhancement you're suggesting could really make our project stand out. Let's explore this further."

Next, Miley from the marketing department shares an idea about how to promote the project. Even though her idea is vastly different from Noah's technical suggestion, you validate her contribution as well: "Thank you for that insight, Miley. Your marketing perspective is crucial to the success of this project. Let's find out how we can integrate this promotional strategy."

Throughout the session, you ensure that everyone's ideas are heard and validated. You facilitate discussions around each idea, encouraging team members to build on each other's suggestions. This encourages the team to be creative, inclusive, and respectful.

By the end of the session, the team will have a list of validated ideas to work with. More importantly, each team member feels valued and heard, developing a positive and collaborative team environment.

In this case, validation was crucial in facilitating a successful brainstorming session. It allowed for a diverse range of ideas to be heard and considered and promoted creativity and inclusiveness. It also helped to build a sense of mutual respect and understanding within the team, which is key to a successful collaborative effort.

#5 – Addressing Employee Burnout: Validating Feelings to Provide Support and Solutions

As a leader, you notice that one of your team members has been showing signs of burnout. They've been working long hours, missing deadlines, and their usual enthusiasm seems to have waned. You decide to address the situation by validating their feelings and providing support and solutions.

1. *Recognize the Signs*: The first step is recognizing the signs

of burnout. This could include changes in behavior, such as increased absenteeism, decreased productivity, or a negative change in attitude.

2. *Initiate a Conversation:* Once you've recognized the signs, the next step is to initiate a conversation. This should be done in a private, non-threatening environment. You might say something like, "I've noticed that you've been working really hard lately and seem to be under a lot of stress. I want to understand how you're feeling and see how we can support you."

3. *Validate Their Feelings:* During the conversation, it's important to validate their feelings. For example, you can say, "It's completely understandable that you're feeling this way. Burnout can happen to anyone, especially when we're working under pressure. Your feelings are valid, and it's important that we address them."

4. *Provide Support:* After validating their feelings, the next step is to provide support. This could involve offering resources for stress management, adjusting their workload, or providing flexibility in their work schedule.

5. *Offer Solutions:* Finally, offer solutions to help prevent burnout in the future. This could involve implementing regular check-ins to discuss workload and stress levels, encouraging work-life balance, or providing training on stress management techniques.

Creating a supportive environment begins with you. When a team member is burned out, offer them empathy through emotional validation and solution-focused assistance.

Exercises and Reflection Points

As we explore further the practical application of emotional valida-tion in professional landscapes, it's time to put theory into practice. The following exercises and reflection points are designed to help you apply the concepts we've discussed in this chapter. They will allow you to explore your understanding of validation, its impact, and its potential in your professional life.

Remember, these exercises and reflection points are not just theoret-ical; they are practical tools that you can use to enhance your profes-sional relationships and foster a more respectful and understanding work environment.

So, grab a pen and a notebook, and take some time to write down your answers. Reflect on them, contemplate your responses, and consider how you can apply these insights in your professional life.

Exercises:

1. *Role-Play Exercise*: Choose one of the scenarios discussed in this chapter and role-play it with a colleague or friend. Take turns playing different roles. This will help you practice applying validation in various professional contexts.

2. *Reflection Exercise*: Think about a recent conflict or challenging situation at your workplace. How could you have used validation to handle the situation more effectively? Write down your thoughts.

3. *Active Listening Exercise*: During your next team meeting or one-on-one conversation, practice active listening. Pay attention to the other person's feelings and needs, and validate them. Notice how this impacts the conversation.

4. *Feedback Exercise*: Practice giving and receiving feedback with a colleague or friend. Remember to focus on the behavior or performance, not the person. Notice how validation can make the feedback more constructive and acceptable.

5. *Burnout Prevention Exercise*: Think about your own needs and boundaries at work. Are they being respected? If not, what steps can you take to address this? Write down your plan.

Reflection Points:

1. Reflect on your role in your professional relationships. How can you use validation to improve these relationships?

2. Consider a time when you felt validated at work. How did it impact your feelings and performance?

3. Think about a time when you didn't feel validated at work. How did it affect you? What could have been done differently?

4. Reflect on the role of validation in team dynamics. How can validation help to resolve conflicts and foster a more inclusive and creative team environment?

5. Consider the role of validation in preventing and addressing burnout. How can you use validation to support your own well-being and the well-being of your colleagues?

My Notes

Chapter Six

Barriers and Solutions

I n this chapter, I will address the various barriers that can hinder the practice of empathy and validation. These barriers can be societal, cultural, or personal, and they can significantly impact our ability to connect with others on a deep, emotional level.

I will discuss the role of biases and prejudices in obstructing genuine connections and how they can be overcome. I will also provide techniques to develop an open mindset and self-awareness, which are crucial for practicing consistent empathy and validation.

Then, you will explore practical scenarios, such as addressing cultural biases in a diverse workplace, to illustrate how these barriers can be overcome in real-life situations. Finally, we will provide exercises and reflection points to help you apply these concepts in your personal and professional life.

By understanding these barriers and learning how to overcome them, you can enhance your ability to be empathetic and affirming in your dealings with others, resulting in deeper, more meaningful relationships.

The Role of Biases in Hindering Genuine Connections

Biases and prejudices, whether they are societal, cultural, or personal, can significantly impede our ability to practice empathy and validation. These preconceived notions can cloud our judgment, leading to misunderstandings and miscommunications and ultimately hindering the formation of genuine connections.

Societal biases, particularly stereotypes, can have a profound impact on our interactions and relationships. These biases are often so deeply ingrained in our societal fabric that we may not even be aware of their influence. Stereotypes, as oversimplified and generalized beliefs about certain groups of people, can lead us to make assumptions that may not align with an individual's reality.

Take the common stereotype that older adults are technologically challenged. While it may hold true for some individuals, this stereotype is by no means a universal truth. There are plenty of older adults who are adept at using technology, and even those who are not can learn with proper guidance and patience. However, the existence of this stereotype can lead to patronizing behavior, where younger individuals might underestimate an older person's ability to handle technology.

This can manifest in various ways. As a case in point, a younger colleague might take over a task involving technology without even asking the older individual if they need help. Or, in a customer service scenario, a representative might automatically assume that an older customer is calling for support because they can't handle a digital interface when the issue might be unrelated to their technological skills.

In both cases, the older adult's abilities and experiences are invalidated, and they are reduced to a stereotype rather than being seen as a unique individual with their own set of skills and experiences. This not only hinders the formation of a genuine connection but can also lead to feelings of frustration and disrespect on the part of the older individual.

Therefore, it's crucial to be aware of these societal biases and make a conscious effort to challenge them, treating each individual as just that – an individual with their own unique set of skills, experiences, and perspectives.

Cultural biases, on the other hand, can stem from differences in customs, traditions, and values across various cultures. These biases can create misunderstandings and hinder the formation of genuine connections. For example, the interpretation of non-verbal cues like eye contact can vary significantly across cultures. In some cultures, maintaining direct eye contact is seen as a sign of respect and attentiveness. It indicates that you are actively listening and are engaged in the conversation.

However, in other cultures, direct eye contact might be considered disrespectful or aggressive. It could be perceived as a challenge or an invasion of personal space. So, if a person from a culture where direct eye contact is valued interacts with someone from a culture where it's considered inappropriate, there can be a significant misunderstanding. The person expecting eye contact might feel ignored or disrespected, while the other person might feel uncomfortable or intimidated.

These cultural biases can extend beyond non-verbal communication to other aspects of interaction as well. For example, certain cultures value direct communication, while others might prefer more indirect and nuanced expressions.

Understanding and acknowledging these cultural differences is crucial in building genuine bonds. We are talking about respecting and validating the other person's cultural norms and communication style, even if they differ from your own. This requires self-awareness, open-mindedness, and a willingness to learn and adapt. It's not about changing who you are but about being respectful and understanding of who the other person is. Top of Form

Personal biases are often the product of our individual experiences, backgrounds, and belief systems. They can significantly shape our perceptions and interactions, sometimes in ways that obstruct the formation of genuine connections. These biases can be towards certain behaviors, professions, or even personal characteristics.

Consider a situation where someone has had a negative experience with a person from a particular profession, say a lawyer. This negative experience might lead them to develop a bias against all lawyers, painting them with the same broad brush. They might start to believe that all lawyers are untrustworthy or manipulative based on their experience with just one individual.

This bias can create a barrier in their interactions with any person they know to be a lawyer. They might approach these interactions with preconceived notions, skepticism, or even hostility. This can prevent them from seeing the individual for who they truly are, separate from their profession. It can hinder them from empathizing with or validating the experiences of these individuals, thereby obstructing the formation of a genuine connection.

Similarly, personal biases can also be based on personal characteristics such as appearance, style of speech, or even lifestyle choices. Namely, someone might have a bias against individuals with tattoos, believing them to be unprofessional or irresponsible. This bias can prevent them from genuinely connecting with individuals who have tattoos, regardless of their actual personality or behavior.

In all these cases, biases and prejudices can be significant barriers to empathy and validation. Overcoming these biases requires self-awareness, introspection, and a conscious effort to separate individuals from our preconceived notions about them. It involves recognizing and challenging our biases and making an effort to understand and connect with individuals based on their unique experiences and perspectives.

Techniques to Foster an Open Mindset and Self-awareness

As we tackle the challenges of biases and prejudices, having an open mind and self-awareness is vital. These aren't just some buzzwords; they're key tools to help us move past our deep-seated biases and truly connect with others. An open mindset allows us to be receptive to new ideas, perspectives, and experiences. It encourages curiosity and learning rather than judgment and stereotyping.

Self-awareness, on the other hand, means recognizing our own biases, emotions, and triggers. It's about understanding how our experiences shape our perceptions and interactions with others.

Now, let's look at some techniques that can help develop an open mindset and self-awareness:

Mindfulness

Mindfulness is about being fully present and engaged in the current moment. It involves observing our thoughts, feelings, and reactions without judgment or immediate reaction. By practicing mindfulness, we can become more aware of our inherent biases and how they might be influencing our thoughts and interactions. Iif you find yourself reacting negatively to a colleague's suggestion, mindfulness can help you pause and examine your reaction. Is it based on the merit of the suggestion, or is it influenced by a bias against the colleague? This awareness can help you respond more objectively and respectfully.

Empathy Mapping

Empathy mapping is an effective technique for cultivating an open mindset. It entails attempting to see the world through another person's eyes. This technique is often used in design thinking but can be applied in any interpersonal context. It is about considering what the other person is seeing, hearing, thinking, and feeling. For example, if a team member is resistant to a new change, instead of dismissing their concerns, you might try to understand their perspective: What are they worried about? What information might they be missing? What is their past experience with similar changes?

This empathy mapping can help you understand their resistance and address it more effectively.

Self-Reflection

Self-reflection serves as a potent instrument for enhancing self-awareness. It requires dedicating time to introspect our thoughts, emotions, actions, and biases. Engaging in regular self-reflection can aid us in identifying our biases and strategizing ways to rectify them. For example, suppose you discern a recurring tendency to undervalue suggestions from less experienced team members. Self-reflection can assist you in probing this bias. What could be the underlying reasons for this tendency? How does it influence your interactions and the overall team synergy? Acknowledging the problem is the initial step toward resolving it.

Or consider a case where you're a customer service representative, and you find yourself getting impatient with customers who aren't tech-savvy. Self-reflection can help you understand this bias. You might ask yourself: Why do I get impatient? Is it because I'm not effectively communicating the instructions? Or is it because I'm not empathizing with their lack of familiarity with technology? How does this impatience affect the quality of service I provide? Acknowledging this bias and understanding its impact is the first step towards improving your interactions with customers.

Seeking Feedback

Inviting feedback from others can be a powerful way to gain insight into our own biases and their impact on our interactions. This process requires a willingness to understand how others view our behaviors and responses. For example, you could approach a respected coworker and ask for their observations on your conduct during team meetings. Are there any noticeable biases in how you engage with different team members? This kind of feedback can offer a fresh viewpoint and assist you in identifying and tackling any unconscious biases.

Continuous Learning

Continuous learning is a proactive pursuit of knowledge, skills, and perspectives. It's about stepping out of your comfort zones and embracing new experiences. This active exploration can help challenge existing beliefs and biases. You might attend workshops or seminars on cultural sensitivity or unconscious bias. These environments provide insights and strategies for addressing biases. Reading books from diverse authors or about different experiences can also broaden your understanding. It allows us to gain a deeper understanding of others' experiences, challenging our preconceived notions.

Engaging in conversations with people from different backgrounds is another effective way to broaden perspectives. These conversations can expose us to different ways of thinking and challenge our biases. Continuous learning also means reflecting on what we've learned and applying it to our interactions. For example, after attending a workshop on cultural sensitivity, you might reflect on how the concepts apply to your workplace and make a conscious effort to apply these learnings. In essence, continuous learning is about transforming knowledge into understanding, empathy, and action. It's about evolving and growing as individuals and professionals, fostering an open mindset, increasing self-awareness, and building genuine, respectful connections.

Overcoming Challenges to Practice Consistent Empathy and Validation

Overcoming challenges to consistently practice empathy and validation is similar to mastering an art. It's about cultivating a mindset that prioritizes understanding and connection, even when faced with situations that might naturally push us towards judgment or indifference. Here's how we can navigate these challenges:

Embrace Curiosity

In a world where snap judgments and rapid conclusions are often the norm, embracing curiosity can be a transformative practice. Instead of letting initial impressions or biases dictate our understanding, we should lean into the unknown with an open heart and mind. When we encounter someone with a differing opinion, rather than dismissing them, we can ask, "Why do you feel that way?" or "Can you tell me more about your experience?"

This not only deepens our understanding but also signals to the other person that their perspective is valued. By developing this sense of wonder and genuine interest in others, we not only enrich our own lives but also create an environment where empathy and connection can flourish. Every person we meet and every situation we encounter holds a lesson; it's up to us to be curious enough to discover it.

Set Empathy Goals

Setting tangible goals is a proven method to achieve growth in various areas of our lives, from physical health to professional achievements. Likewise, when it comes to nurturing our empathetic side, setting clear, actionable goals can be immensely beneficial. For instance, you might decide that every Monday during your lunch break, you'll engage with a colleague you haven't spoken to in depth before. The aim? To understand more about their weekend activities or their passion projects outside of work.

Another goal could be to dedicate one meeting a week where you consciously refrain from interrupting anyone, ensuring you fully absorb what's being shared before formulating a response. By the end of the month, you might aim to have four meaningful conversations you wouldn't have had otherwise or to have improved your active listening skills in several meetings. These small, intentional actions can bring a more empathetic disposition and enhanced interpersonal relationships.

Journaling for Awareness

The simple act of journaling can be a mirror to our souls, reflecting our deepest emotions and reactions. For example, you might note that during a team meeting, a colleague's comment made you feel defensive. Upon reflection, you realize it reminded you of a past experience where your idea was dismissed. Or imagine, you're out for a walk in your neighborhood. You come across a neighbor's child trying to fix a broken toy. You stop, kneel down, and spend a few minutes helping the child.

Later, when you journal about this seemingly small event, you realize it brought back memories of your own childhood when you longed for someone to notice and help you. Another day, you might write about the warmth you felt when a stranger in the grocery store shared a genuine smile with you, reminding you of the interconnectedness of humanity. As days turn into weeks and you continue this practice, you'll uncover layers of emotions, triggers, and joys that you might have otherwise overlooked.

This self-awareness can be a guiding light, helping you navigate life with more empathy and understanding, not just for others but for yourself as well. Through journaling, you're not just documenting moments; it is beyond that; it initiates an exploration of the self, encouraging profound connections to the surrounding context.

Engage in Role Reversal

One of the most transformative ways to foster empathy is by momentarily stepping out of our own viewpoint and stepping into someone else's. Let's consider a relatable example: you're in a heated discussion with a friend who seems unreasonably upset about a change in weekend plans. You remember that they recently mentioned feeling overwhelmed at work and having sleepless nights due to personal issues.

Instead of reacting defensively to their frustration, you take a moment to think about their current emotional state. Perhaps they've had a stressful week, or they were genuinely looking forward to the original plan as a brief escape from their challenges. By mentally switching roles, you can gain insights into potential fears, stresses, or emotions driving their reactions. It's not about justifying or agreeing with their behavior but understanding it.

This understanding can be the bridge to a more constructive conversation. Over time, practicing role reversal in various situations, from disagreements with family members to misunderstandings with colleagues, can help cultivate a more empathetic and understanding approach to interactions, reducing conflicts and enhancing relationships.

Limit Exposure to Negativity

In today's digital age, we're constantly bombarded with information, and not all of it is uplifting. Continual exposure to negative stimuli can desensitize us or make us more cynical. It's essential to be selective about what we consume and with whom we spend our time. When it comes to news consumption, while it's crucial to stay informed, it's equally vital to ensure that the news doesn't overwhelm you. Instead of starting your day with distressing headlines, perhaps begin with a motivational podcast or a light-hearted read. Allocate specific times in the day to catch up on the news rather than having it as a constant background noise.

Social media platforms can sometimes become echo chambers of negativity. Consider decluttering your feed and following accounts that inspire and uplift you. If you love art, for example, follow galleries or artists who show their work, pushing the negative chatter down your feed.

In our personal lives, we sometimes encounter those who thrive on negativity or drama. Though we can't always avoid these interactions entirely, we can limit them or steer conversations to more uplifting territory. To give you an idea, if a complaining colleague fixates on work problems, suggest discussing a movie or hobby instead.

Consciously curating your environment this way creates space for empathy to grow. By surrounding yourself with positivity when possible, you're better able to approach any situation with patience, balance and compassion. A nurturing personal landscape allows understanding to flourish.

Joining Empathy Circles

Deepening our understanding of others often requires stepping out of our comfort zones and actively listening to diverse narratives. Empathy circles provide just the platform for this. These are nurturing spaces where individuals from different walks of life converge to share their personal journeys, challenges, and triumphs. The primary objective isn't to advise or solve but to listen, comprehend, and connect on a profound level. Consider attending an empathy circle where a young entrepreneur speaks about the rollercoaster of starting a business, the sleepless nights, the small victories, and the lessons learned from failures.

In the same setting, a retired teacher might reflect on the evolving education system, reminiscing about chalkboards and handwritten notes and expressing the challenges of adapting to online teaching tools during her last years of service. Another participant could share the journey of adopting a child, the anticipation, the hurdles, and the boundless joy of becoming a parent.

Listening to these varied narratives not only offers a window into different worlds but also challenges our biases and expands our horizons. It's one thing to read about the challenges of entrepreneurship, but it's entirely different to hear it directly from someone who has lived and experienced it, to witness their passion, and to resonate with their determination.

Furthermore, empathy circles serve as an opportunity for personal reflection. Sharing your own narrative, unveiling your fears, and feeling validated can be a healing experience. It underscores the idea that while our stories might differ, the underlying emotions - be it excitement, apprehension, joy, or determination - are universally relatable. In addition, joining these kinds of groups, like local community circles, online forums, or school settings, can help create a more empathetic and comprehending community.

Continuous Learning

The world is vast, filled with diverse cultures, histories, and personal stories. By dedicating time to understanding these varied experiences, we can broaden our perspectives and reduce biases. Reading about different cultures, watching documentaries on influential movements, or engaging in conversations with individuals from diverse backgrounds can be enlightening. This isn't just about gathering information but truly understanding different viewpoints. It helps us see beyond labels, recognizing the dreams, challenges, and aspirations of others. At its core, continuous learning cultivates a more informed and inclusive worldview.

Practicing Active Feedback

Feedback is a powerful tool for growth and self-improvement. It's like holding up a mirror to our actions and behaviors, showing us how we're perceived by others. This can be particularly useful when it comes to understanding and managing our biases. By regularly seeking feedback from those around us, we can gain valuable insights into how our actions and words are interpreted.

Think about a domestic scenario where you and your teenage child are often at odds. You feel like you're being reasonable, but your child seems to be constantly upset with you. In this case, asking for feedback can be incredibly helpful. You might sit down with your child and ask them how they perceive your interactions. Do they feel understood and respected? Are there instances where they felt you were dismissive or not fully understanding their point of view?

While it may be challenging to hear, this feedback can provide a more objective view of your interactions. It can highlight instances where your biases or preconceived notions might have influenced your behavior, allowing you to recognize and remedy these issues.

Celebrating Small Wins

Progress is often made up of small, incremental steps, and it's important to acknowledge and celebrate these moments. Every time you successfully practice empathy or validation, especially in challenging situations, take a moment to recognize your achievement. This celebration acts as a positive boost, motivating the continuation of such behavior.

Imagine you have a friend who often shares their problems with you. In the past, you might have jumped straight into problem-solving mode, offering advice and solutions. But this time, you make a conscious effort to simply listen and validate their feelings. You resist the urge to 'fix' their problem and instead, just offer a listening ear and empathetic responses. This is a win worth acknowledging! You've successfully practiced empathy and validation and likely made your friend feel heard and understood.

In a professional context, imagine you're in charge of a team meeting. One of your team members, who is usually quiet, shares an idea. Instead of moving on quickly, you take the time to validate their contribution, acknowledging the thought and effort that went into it. You ask them to expand on their idea, encouraging further discussion. This not only validates the team member but also helps promote an inclusive environment where everyone feels valued. Recognizing and celebrating this moment reinforces your commitment to empathy and validation in the workplace.

By incorporating these practices into our daily routines, we can significantly improve our personal relationships and facilitate a more empathetic and understanding society. This journey, filled with continuous growth and learning, brings us closer to forming genuine connections and enriching our interactions with others. Moreover, these practices extend beyond our immediate circles. They help bridge gaps, challenge stereotypes, and promote understanding among diverse groups. Remember, it's about making a conscious effort every day to understand and validate the feelings of others, thereby contributing to a more compassionate world.

Practice Scenario: Addressing Cultural Biases in a Diverse Workplace

John, a project manager, leads a diverse team comprising members from various cultural backgrounds. The team includes Maria from Mexico, Ahmed from Egypt, and Li from China. They are working on a project that requires close collaboration and effective communication.

John notices that during team meetings, Ahmed and Li are often quiet and don't contribute much to the discussions. Maria, on the other hand, is very vocal and often dominates the conversation. John also observes that Ahmed and Li seem uncomfortable when Maria speaks directly and assertively, which is a communication style common in her culture.

John realizes that cultural biases might be hindering effective communication and collaboration within his team. He recognizes that he needs to address this issue to ensure a harmonious and productive work environment.

Exercises and Reflection Points

The exercises and reflection points that follow are designed to help you apply the concepts we've discussed in this chapter to a real-world situation. They will challenge you to think critically, empathize with the characters, and develop actionable strategies to address cultural biases.

Remember, the goal is not just to understand the scenario but to reflect on your own experiences and biases. So, grab a pen and a notebook to jot down your answers and reflections, and let's get started.

Exercises:

1. *Identify the cultural biases*: Reflect on the scenario. What cultural biases are at play here? How are they affecting the team dynamics?

2. *Empathize with the team members*: Put yourself in the shoes of each team member. How might they be feeling? What challenges might they be facing due to these cultural differ-

ences?

3. *Develop an action plan:* As John, what steps would you take to address these cultural biases and improve team dynamics? Consider the techniques discussed earlier, such as fostering an open mindset, seeking feedback, and practicing empathy.

Reflection Points:

1. *Reflect on your own experiences:* Have you ever faced a similar situation in your personal or professional life? How did you handle it? What did you learn from that experience?

2. *Set empathy goals:* Based on this scenario, set some empathy goals for yourself. What specific actions will you take in the next week to practice empathy and validation in your interactions?

3. *Cultural Sensitivity:* Think about a time when you were in a culturally diverse environment. Were there any misunderstandings or conflicts that arose due to cultural differences? How did you handle the situation?

4. *Identify Your Own Biases:* Reflect on your own biases. Are there certain cultures or groups of people you have preconceived notions about? How might these biases be influencing your interactions and relationships?

5. *Improvement Areas:* Based on your reflections, identify one area where you could improve your empathy and validation skills. What specific actions could you take to work on this area?

My Notes

Chapter Seven

Empathy in the Digital Age

T he digital era, characterized by the swift transition to virtual interactions, has fundamentally reshaped our communication patterns and interpersonal dynamics. This shift from in-person to screen-mediated communication has redefined the way we express, perceive, and interpret emotions. The subtleties of human emotions, previously conveyed through physical presence, tone of voice, and body language, are now often encapsulated in text messages, emails, and social media posts. This transformation has introduced new challenges in practicing empathy and validation as we navigate the digital landscape.

However, this shift is not solely about challenges. It also gives us unique opportunities to practice empathy and validation on a broader scale. With its global reach and instantaneous communication, the digital world enables us to interact with people from varied cultures, grasp alternative viewpoints, and build a shared community spirit. To seize these opportunities, we need to adapt our empathetic skills to the digital context, learn to decipher emotions from text, respond empathetically in online interactions, and validate experiences shared across digital platforms.

In this chapter, we will explore the nuances of empathy in our increasingly digital world together. I will provide you with practical techniques to discern emotions and intentions in digital interactions and discuss the unique challenges that arise when trying to convey empathy and validation online. We will also look at the role of social media in shaping our empathetic responses and how it can be used as a tool for understanding and connection.

I will present you with forward-thinking strategies to cultivate authentic connections in the digital sphere and provide a practical scenario to guide you in managing a heated disagreement on social media. To help you integrate these concepts into your daily life, I will offer exercises and reflection points that encourage active engagement and personal growth.

Our goal in this chapter is to equip you with the knowledge and tools necessary to navigate the digital realm with empathy and understanding. So you can expect to enhance your digital interactions and relationships, building a more empathetic and inclusive online community through this chapter.

Recognizing Emotions and Intent in Digital Interactions

Recognizing emotions and intent in digital interactions is a nuanced process that requires a keen understanding of both verbal and non-verbal cues. In the digital realm, we don't have the advantage of observing facial expressions or hearing voice inflections, which are key elements in face-to-face communication. Instead, we rely heavily on written language, emojis, and other digital expressions to convey and interpret emotions.

Imagine an email exchange with a colleague. The words that they used, the tone, the length of the sentences, and even the punctuation can give us clues about their emotional state. A short, terse response might indicate frustration, impatience, or even a lack of interest or attention. An email filled with exclamation points and emojis might suggest excitement or enthusiasm.

Similarly, in a text conversation, the use of emojis, GIFs, and stickers can provide valuable insights into a person's emotions. A smiley face or a heart emoji can express happiness or affection, while a sad face or a thumbs down might indicate disappointment or disapproval.

However, it's important to remember that these are just indicators, not definitive proof of someone's emotional state. Sure, digital communication lacks the richness of face-to-face interactions, and there's always a risk of misinterpretation. For example, a colleague or a friend might use short sentences in their emails simply because they prefer concise communication, not because they're upset or annoyed.

Recognizing intent in digital interactions can be even more challenging. Intent refers to what a person wants to achieve with their communication. It's about understanding the purpose behind their words. For example, if a team member sends a long, detailed email about a project, their intent might be to keep everyone informed and ensure transparency. On the other hand, a friend sending a funny meme might be trying to lighten your day.

Nowadays, where face-to-face interactions are often replaced by emails, texts, and social media posts, developing the ability to recognize emotions and intent in digital interactions is crucial. It helps us respond appropriately, build better relationships, and navigate the digital world with empathy and understanding.

Challenges in Conveying Empathy and Validation Online

In the digital era, the lack of physical cues and the risk of misunderstanding make showing empathy online challenging. However, by identifying these issues and adopting specific strategies, we can improve our digital connections.

Absence of Non-Verbal Cues

The absence of non-verbal cues in digital interactions could potentially create challenges and difficulties. In face-to-face interactions, we rely heavily on non-verbal cues such as facial expressions, body language, and tone of voice to understand others' emotions and intentions. In digital interactions, these cues are often absent, making it harder to recognize and respond to others' feelings. For example, a text message or email can be interpreted in many different ways depending on the reader's mood or assumptions, leading to potential misunderstandings.

However, there are ways to navigate this challenge. One method is to be more explicit in our written communication. If you're sending an email, you could specify your emotions or intentions in the text. You might say, "I'm writing this with a smile," or "I'm feeling concerned about...". This can help convey your emotional state to the reader and reduce misunderstandings to a great extent.

In video calls, we can still use some non-verbal cues like facial expressions and gestures. To illustrate, nodding along when someone is speaking can show that you're listening and engaged, or it could mean that you find what they are saying interesting. Tilting your head can also affirm your interest, as this gesture is often interpreted as a way to "lend your ear."

Remember that these strategies may not work in all situations or for everyone. Some people may not be comfortable using emojis, while others may interpret them differently. Equally, non-verbal cues in video calls can be missed due to technical issues or if the video is turned off. Therefore, it's crucial to be mindful of these limitations and adjust our communication strategies accordingly.

For example, if you're on a video call with a colleague and notice that they seem distracted or upset, you might send them a private message after the call to check in. You could say, "I noticed that you seemed a bit distracted during our call. Is everything okay?" This shows that you're paying attention to their non-verbal cues and that you care about their well-being, thereby conveying empathy and validation.

While the absence of non-verbal cues in digital interactions can create challenges, there are strategies we can use to convey empathy and validation. By being more explicit in our communication, using emojis or emoticons, and paying attention to non-verbal cues in video calls, we can help bridge the gap and build more empathetic digital interactions.

Potential for Misinterpretation

The potential for misinterpretation is really a significant challenge in digital communication. Without the context provided by non-verbal cues, our messages can be easily misunderstood. A joke might be taken as an insult, or a simple statement might be perceived as aggressive. This is especially true in text-based communication, where tone of voice and facial expressions are absent.

Reflect on this situation where you send a text to a friend, and you say, "We need to talk." Such a statement, in the absence of context, can stir anxiety and uncertainty. Your friend might wonder if they've done something wrong or if there's bad news awaiting them. In other words, without any additional context or cues, your friend might interpret this message as ominous or serious, even if you just wanted to discuss weekend plans!

In our daily rush to get things done, we might send a short, concise email to a colleague. But without realizing it, that brevity might come off as curt or even dismissive. Imagine you're on the receiving end of an email that just says, "Send the report by noon." It feels a bit cold, doesn't it? A simple tweak, like "Could you please send the report by noon? Thanks!" adds a touch of warmth and understanding. Isn't it incredible how just a few extra words can change the entire tone of a message?

That's why it's so important to be mindful of how our words might be interpreted. For example, using clear, direct language can help reduce misunderstandings. Instead of saying, "We need to talk," you could say, "Can we chat about our weekend plans?" This provides context and reduces the potential for misinterpretation.

You can also use emojis or emoticons to convey tone and emotion. A smiley face or a thumbs-up can help indicate a positive tone, while a sad face or a thumbs-down can express disappointment or disagreement. However, it's important to use these symbols appropriately and consider the other person's comfort level with them.

In professional settings, it can be helpful to add a note of appreciation or a positive comment in your emails. This can set a positive tone and reduce the chances of your message being perceived as harsh or dismissive. For example, you could start your email with "I appreciate your work on this project" before providing feedback or asking for changes.

Finally, when in doubt, it's always a good idea to ask for clarification. If you're unsure about the tone or intent of a message you received, you could respond with something like, "I want to make sure I'm understanding you correctly. Are you saying...?" This shows that you're making an effort to understand their perspective, which is a crucial aspect of empathy.

Volume of Interactions

The digital age has indeed expanded our capacity to connect with more people than ever before. This increased connectivity, however, also means we're dealing with a higher volume of interactions. This could create complications when it comes to providing each interaction with the level of empathy and validation it deserves.

Take the example of a customer service representative. In a single day, they might be dealing with hundreds of customer queries, each with its unique concerns and emotions. The representative needs to understand the customer's issue, empathize with their frustration, and provide a solution, all within a few minutes. This rapid-moving, heavy-traffic setting can render it difficult to uphold a steady level of empathy.

Correspondingly, a manager in a large organization might find it difficult to empathize with each team member's concerns when they're managing a large team spread across different time zones. The sheer volume of interactions and the diversity of issues can make it tough to provide individualized empathy and validation.

To navigate this challenge, it's important to have strategies in place to handle the volume of interactions without compromising on empathy. One approach is to prioritize quality over quantity. Instead of trying to respond to all messages immediately, take the time to understand each situation and respond thoughtfully. This could mean responding to fewer messages in a day, but the quality of your responses will likely be higher.

Of course, you can also use specific tools and techniques to manage your interactions. For example, customer service representatives might use templates for common queries, which they can then personalize for each customer. They might also use customer relationship management (CRM) systems to track customer interactions and ensure each customer feels heard and valued.

In a managerial context, regular one-on-one meetings with team members can provide a dedicated space for empathy and validation. These meetings can help managers understand each team member's unique challenges and provide personalized support. By prioritizing quality over quantity, using appropriate tools and techniques, and creating dedicated spaces for empathy, we can manage our digital interactions more effectively and empathetically.

Anonymity and Disinhibition

The digital landscape often provides a veil of anonymity, which can lead to a phenomenon known as online disinhibition. This is where individuals express themselves more freely and intensely than they would in face-to-face interactions. While this can sometimes lead to open and honest discussions, it can also result in aggressive or disrespectful behavior, making it hard to respond empathetically.

Consider the setting of an online class, a space designed for learning and growth. Students are prompted to join discussion forums, adding their insights and queries to have a collective educational experience. The vast majority, recognizing the shared goal of enlightenment, contribute thoughtfully and respectfully. Yet, there's often that one individual, fortified by the veil of online anonymity, who chooses a different path. Instead of constructive input, they might scatter disruptive or even offensive remarks, like seeds sown to create discord. Such actions aren't merely distractions; they act as barriers, challenging the course's very objectives. They divert the conversation from its intended path, creating detours filled with needless confrontation.

Moreover, this kind of behavior instigates a ripple effect. An antagonistic comment might make others hesitant to participate, fearing backlash or mockery. The once collaborative and open forum transforms into a battlefield of words, with many students opting for the sidelines rather than risking engagement. In these situations, extending compassion and empathy towards the disruptor becomes an uphill task. It demands instructors and fellow students to dig deep, look beyond the surface-level chaos and perhaps seek an understanding of the underlying causes of such behavior, all while maintaining the purpose of the educational space.

On social media platforms, it's not uncommon for users to cross paths with trolls. These are individuals who seem to derive a perverse pleasure from posting incendiary or outright offensive content, all with the goal of triggering intense reactions. Their motives often aren't rooted in genuine belief or feeling but rather in the chaos and discomfort they can generate.

Addressing such behavior with empathy is a tall order, especially when you consider that a troll's main objective isn't to cultivate understanding or constructive discourse. Instead, they're on a mission to disrupt, sidetracking meaningful conversations and often making platforms feel like hostile environments. The digital veil provides them an anonymity that encourages this behavior, further emphasizing the importance of approaching online interactions with caution and discernment.

In professional circles, have you ever noticed how the digital curtain sometimes makes us a bit bolder? It's like, when we're not face-to-face, some of the usual filters just drop. Think about a virtual team meeting. Without seeing a colleague's immediate reaction or body language, someone might just blurt out criticisms or brush aside an idea without thinking about the feelings on the other end. It's easy to forget there's a real person behind that screen when you're just staring at a username or a profile picture. So, just as we'd tread carefully in person, it's super important to remember that touch of kindness and understanding, even in the virtual world.

To address these challenges, it's important to establish clear guidelines for digital interactions, whether it's in an online class, a social media platform, or a virtual meeting. These guidelines should promote respectful and constructive dialogue and discourage disruptive behavior.

When encountering aggressive or disrespectful behavior, it's crucial to respond calmly and assertively. Instead of engaging in a heated exchange, acknowledge the person's feelings but also express your own. Namely, you might say, "I understand that you're upset, but it's important that we communicate respectfully."

In some cases, it might be necessary to involve a moderator or supervisor to address the disruptive behavior. Keep this in mind, while empathy means understanding others' feelings, it doesn't mean tolerating disrespect or aggression.

Cultural Differences

The global reach of the internet means we're often interacting with people from a wide array of cultures and backgrounds. This cultural diversity, while enriching, can also lead to misunderstandings and miscommunications if we're not mindful. Cultural nuances, varying social norms, and different interpretations of language and symbols can all play a role in these misunderstandings.

Picture a group of friends from different parts of the world who communicate primarily through a messaging app. A phrase or an emoji that one friend uses casually, considering it friendly or humorous, might be seen as inappropriate or offensive by another friend from a different cultural background. For example, the thumbs-up emoji is regarded as a positive gesture in many Western cultures, but did you know that in some Middle Eastern cultures, it can be seen as a disrespectful sign?

Likewise, in an online class with students from various cultural backgrounds, a comment that seems harmless to some might be perceived as insensitive by others. A student might share an opinion or a joke that, while considered acceptable in their culture, could be offensive or inappropriate in another culture.

In professional settings, too, cultural differences can lead to misunderstandings. A business email that seems straightforward and professional to a team member in one country might come across as cold or impersonal to a colleague in another country, where a more personal and friendly tone is the norm.

To navigate these cultural differences, it's essential to cultivate cultural sensitivity and awareness, which means learning about different cultures, being mindful of potential cultural pitfalls, and being open to feedback. If you're unsure how a message might come across, it's a good idea to play it safe and pick your words and emojis thoughtfully.

When misunderstandings occur, approach them with a willingness to learn. Apologize if necessary, clarify your intent, and take the opportunity to learn more about the other person's culture. Over time, this openness and willingness to learn can help build stronger, more understanding connections in the digital world.

By acknowledging these challenges, we pave the way for the development of strategies and techniques that can enhance our ability to convey empathy and validation in our digital interactions. This recognition is not merely about identifying the obstacles but also about understanding their implications and how they can be addressed. It's about transforming these challenges into opportunities for growth, learning, and improved communication.

Social Media: Addressing and Navigating Online Conflicts and Misunderstandings

Navigating the realm of social media can be a complex task, especially when it comes to expressing empathy and validation. The digital landscape, with its unique dynamics, presents a new set of challenges and opportunities for empathetic communication.

One of the primary aspects of empathy in social media is addressing and navigating online conflicts and misunderstandings. The virtual nature of these platforms can sometimes amplify disagreements due to the lack of non-verbal cues and the potential for misinterpretation. However, with a conscious effort and the right strategies, we can use these platforms to promote understanding and resolve conflicts effectively.

Let's consider a few cases:

Online Debates

Social media platforms are often a hotbed for debates on various topics. While these discussions can be enriching, they can also quickly escalate into heated arguments. In such situations, it's crucial to remember the principles of empathy. Instead of focusing on winning the argument, try to understand the other person's perspective. Ask clarifying questions, acknowledge their points, and express your views respectfully.

To give you an idea, if you're engaged in a debate about climate change, instead of dismissing someone who holds a different opinion, try to understand their viewpoint. Ask them about the sources of their information and share your resources. This approach not only encourages a more constructive conversation but also opens the door for mutual learning.

Responding to Negative Comments

Negative comments or feedback can be challenging to handle. It's natural to feel defensive, but responding impulsively can escalate the situation. Instead, take a moment to understand the person's perspective. Are they upset about a specific issue? Is there a misunderstanding that needs to be clarified? Responding with empathy can help de-escalate the situation and lead to a more productive conversation.

For example, if you're managing a business's social media account and receive a complaint about a product, resist the urge to be defensive. Instead, acknowledge the customer's dissatisfaction, apologize if necessary, and offer a solution. This approach shows that you value the customer's experience and are committed to resolving their issues.

Sharing and Responding to Personal Experiences

Social media platforms are often used to share personal experiences, thoughts, and feelings. Responding to these posts with empathy can build deeper connections and provide support to those who need it.

Suppose a friend shares a post about struggling with mental health. Instead of simply reacting to the post, you could leave a supportive comment acknowledging their courage to share such a personal experience and offering your support. This simple act can go a long way in making the person feel seen, heard, and validated.

Coming up, we'll go over effective strategies to help you make genuine connections in the digital world. These strategies will equip you with the tools to not only navigate the digital landscape but also to build and maintain meaningful relationships, regardless of the medium.

How to Cultivate Genuine Connections Online

The digital age, while providing us with unprecedented connectivity, has also presented us with unique challenges in making real connections. In particular, the absence of physical presence and non-verbal cues, as we discussed previously, can make it difficult to convey and interpret emotions accurately. However, by understanding these challenges and adopting specific strategies, we can enhance our ability to empathize and validate in the digital realm, thereby enriching our online interactions.

A fundamental strategy is acknowledging our shared human nature. Online, it's tempting to present an idealized version of ourselves, hiding behind the safety of our screens. However, this can create a barrier to authentic connection. When we're honest about our insecurities, achievements, and challenges, it allows for deeper, more authentic bonds with others. This level of authenticity, this willingness to share our real nature, can resonate deeply with others, encouraging them to do the same and laying the groundwork for more meaningful connections.

Understanding the nuances of different communication channels is another crucial strategy. Each form of digital communication, be it emails, texts, or instant messages, serves a unique purpose and is suited to different types of conversations. Quick updates or simple questions might be effectively handled through a text message, but for more complex or sensitive discussions, a phone call or video chat might be more appropriate. Recognizing when to switch from one mode of communication to another can help prevent misunderstandings and convey empathy more effectively.

Authenticity is so important on social media today. Amidst all the filtered posts and idealized feeds, we can't lose sight of the worth of true connections. This happens through exchanging substantial moments, having thoughtful dialogues, and taking a sincere interest in people. Don't get caught up in likes or followers - instead, build bonds grounded in mutual respect and compassion. Focus on developing rapport through under-standing, not superficial validations. When we share openly and engage mindfully, we invite others to do the same in their own way. That's how authenticity prospers online.

Lastly, offering your time, skills, or expertise can be a powerful way to build connections. Whether it's helping a colleague with a project, sharing useful resources within your network, or volunteering for a cause you care about, these acts of service can establish a foundation of trust and mutual respect. They demonstrate your willingness to invest in the relationship, which is a vital element of a genuine connection.

Practice Scenario: Responding to a Heated Disagreement on Social Media

Picture this: You are part of a book club group on a social media platform. The group is discussing a popular novel, and a heated disagreement arises about the interpretation of the main character's actions in the book. One group member, Benjamin, firmly believes that the character's actions were justified given the circumstances in the story. Another member, Thomas, disagrees and argues that the character acted selfishly and without respect for others. The discussion quickly escalates, with Benjamin and Thomas trading increasingly harsh comments.

As this case demonstrates, even those with shared interests can experience conflict when interpretations differ. With empathy and emotional validation skills now in your toolkit, how might you help diffuse disagreement and facilitate understanding if you were part of this book club?

Exercises and Reflection Points

Now, let's move on to the exercises and reflection points. Make sure to use a notebook to journal your thoughts and reflections as you go through these exercises. Reflecting on these points can help you to better understand and apply empathy and validation in your digital interactions.

Exercises:

1. *Identify the Emotions:* What emotions might Benjamin and Thomas be feeling during this disagreement? How might these emotions influence their responses to each other?

2. *Practice Empathetic Responses:* Write down how you might respond to both Benjamin and Thomas in an empathetic

and validating way. Consider how you might acknowledge their feelings, validate their perspectives, and help reduce the tension.

3. *Consider the Impact of Tone:* How might the tone of Benjamin and Thomas's comments contribute to the escalation of the disagreement? How could a change in tone potentially change the course of the conversation?

Reflection Points:

Now, let's move on to some reflection points:

1. *Reflect on Your Own Experiences:* Have you ever been in a similar situation where a disagreement escalated on social media? How did you handle it? What might you do differently in the future?

2. *Consider the Role of Empathy:* How might empathy and validation change the course of Benjamin and Thomas's disagreement? How could these skills improve your own online interactions?

3. *Think About the Challenges:* What challenges might you face in trying to convey empathy and validation in a heated online disagreement? How might you overcome these challenges?

Chapter Eight

Cultivating Vulnerable, Fulfilling Relationships

O pening up and sharing the real us - that's another key to making deep, heartfelt connections. Being vulnerable takes courage. It means letting people into our innermost thoughts and feelings, even the messy or scary stuff we keep private. But dropping our guard doesn't reveal weakness - it shows our humanity and strength. When we can be authentic without walls or masks, it permits others to do the same. Vulnerability is about embracing all of who we are, uncertainties and all, and saying, "I accept myself as I am." That raw honesty breeds the kind of intimacy and understanding that creates profound bonds.

This openness, this willingness to be seen, serves as a bridge, allowing trust to form and deepen. It signals to others that we are not only open to their experiences and perspectives but also value them. It's a reciprocal process where our openness encourages others to be open as well, creating a cycle of empathy and validation.

We'll look at how empathy and validating others help build trust. You'll learn tactics for having meaningful interactions and creating relationships based on mutual respect and understanding. I will also provide a practice scenario that involves opening up about personal struggles in a relationship, followed by exercises and reflection points to help you apply these concepts in your daily life. The aim is to guide you in cultivating relationships that are not only fulfilling but also enriching and transformative.

Forging Bonds of Trust Through Understanding

Trust is the bedrock upon which strong relationships are con-structed. But building robust trust requires more than surface level interactions. It calls for showing up fully - mind, body and spirit. Through compassionate listening and emotional attunement, we can create sanctuaries of understanding where vulnerability is wel-comed, not feared. This is the alchemy of empathy and validation at work.

When we offer someone the gift of our wholehearted attention, we nurture trust. Listen with not just the ears, but the heart. Make space for their truth without judgment. Validate emotions that may seem irrational to you, but are excruciatingly real for them. Don't just hear words - feel the meaning behind them.

Show the strength of your bond by absorbing their storms when the deluge comes, without collapsing. Help dry their tears without drowning in them.

Imagine a scenario involving two friends, Jacob and Thomas. Jacob has been going through a tough time at work, feeling overwhelmed and stressed. He decides to share his feelings with Thomas, hoping to find a listening ear and some comfort. Thomas, in response, acknowledges Jacob's feelings, validates his experience, and expresses his understanding. This empathetic response from Thomas makes Jacob feel heard and understood, reinforcing the trust between them.

In this case, empathy and validation serve as catalysts for trust. They create a safe environment where vulnerability is welcomed and cherished. This trust, once established, becomes the foundation for a deeper connection, nurturing a relationship grounded not in superficiality but in shared comprehension and respect.

Trust blossoms when people sense you are rooted in their reality, not yours. You accept them as they are, with an open heart, not an open agenda. Promises can be broken, but understanding endures. This compassion is not finite, but an infinite renewable resource. Generate trust by validating and revalidating. Understand and keep seeking to understand more deeply. Forge bonds too strong to sever through the empathy that knows no end. This is the trust that transforms relationships.

Guidelines for Real and Effective Interactions

As we move forward from understanding the role of empathy and validation in establishing trust, we now turn our attention to the strategies that can help us engage in meaningful and reciprocal interactions. These strategies are not just about having conversations; they are about creating connections that are deep, fulfilling, and mutually beneficial.

Being attentive is crucial for meaningful and reciprocal interactions. This means actively listening to what the other person is saying, showing interest in their thoughts and feelings, and responding in a way that shows you understand and value their perspective. For example, if a friend is sharing their experiences about a challenging situation at work, being attentive means not just hearing their words but also recognizing the emotions behind those words and responding in a supportive and understanding manner.

Another approach is to be caring and warm in our interactions which means showing kindness, care, and concern for the other person. It means making the other person feel valued and appreciated. For example, if a friend is going through a tough time, being nurturing could mean offering words of encouragement, providing a listening ear, or simply being there for them in their time of need.

Being responsive is also crucial in engaging in meaningful interactions. This means not just listening to what the other person is saying but also responding in a way that shows you understand and care about their feelings and experiences. Such as, if your sister shares a concern with you, being responsive could mean offering advice, providing reassurance, or simply acknowledging their feelings.

In meaningful interactions, treating others with dignity and consideration is key to showing respect. Specifically, during disagreements, this involves listening to the other person's viewpoint, avoiding personal attacks, and working toward a mutually beneficial resolution.

Guiding and following the other person's lead is another strategy that can foster meaningful interactions. This means being flexible in our interactions, allowing the other person to guide the conversation at times, and stepping in to guide when necessary. If a colleague is opening up about a personal issue, you might follow their lead in the conversation, allowing them to share at their own pace. At the same time, you might also guide the conversation by asking open-ended questions that encourage them to express their feelings and thoughts.

In the next part, we'll explore hands-on ways to create bonds of mutual respect and understanding. I'll share approaches you can use to cultivate deeper connections in your relationships.

Fundamentals of Respectful Relationships

In the sphere of relationships, mutual respect and understanding form the cornerstone that supports the construction of strong and enduring connections. These elements are not just about acknowledging the other person's existence or their role in your life but about valuing their individuality, their experiences, their perspectives, and their emotions. It's about seeing the other person as they truly are, without judgment or preconceived notions, and accepting them wholeheartedly.

When we talk about fostering relationships rooted in mutual respect and understanding, we're talking about creating an environment where both parties feel seen, heard, and valued. This is not a one-time effort but a continuous process that requires conscious and consistent effort. It's about being present, open, and willing to engage in meaningful and sometimes difficult conversations.

One of the critical aspects of fostering such relationships is the ability to communicate effectively. Communication is not just about expressing your thoughts and feelings but also about listening to understand the other person's perspective. It's about creating a safe space where both parties can express themselves freely and honestly without fear of judgment or rejection.

Now, let's look at a case between two friends, Maria and Lisa. Maria is passionate about environmental conservation and often participates in activities like beach cleanups and tree planting events. Lisa doesn't share the same enthusiasm for environmentalism, but she respects Maria's dedication to the cause.

When Maria returns from a recent beach cleanup, brimming with stories about the day, Lisa sets aside time to hear all about it over coffee. "It looked like a completely different beach after just a few hours of cleaning up trash!" Maria says. "I'm amazed by how much waste washes up."

"Wow, that's really cool that you're making such an impact," Lisa replies. "Are you noticing any changes on the beach since you started these cleanups?"

Maria smiles, grateful that Lisa takes an interest in something important to her. She launches into details about the reduction in plastics and debris. Lisa continues asking questions and listening intently, even suggesting Maria expand her work by starting an environmental club at their university.

While Lisa may never join one of the beach cleanups herself, she understands Maria's dedication is making a tangible difference. By engaging with openness and respect for her friend's passion, Lisa nurtures their bond. Her curiosity and validation, even without sharing the same interest, means so much to Maria.

Boundaries are essential for maintaining a healthy relationship as they define the limits of what is acceptable and what is not. Respecting boundaries means understanding and accepting that there are certain things that the other person is not comfortable with and avoiding those actions or behaviors. For example, Boundaries are crucial for maintaining healthy workplace relationships. Let's look at a scenario between coworkers James and Samira to understand this further.

James and Samira have adjacent desks and often chat casually as they work. James usually shares funny tidbits about his kids or weekend hiking trips. Samira laughs along politely, but tends to keep details of her personal life private during work hours.

One Monday, James asks Samira how her date went over the weekend. Feeling this crosses a line into her private life, Samira gently responds, "You know, I prefer to keep my personal life separate. But I appreciate you taking an interest!"

While James' intention was friendly small talk, Samira establishes it is a boundary for her. The next time James asks an overly personal question, Samira firmly reiterates her preference to keep work and personal separate.

Showing irritation or anger would likely only breed resentment. Samira makes her boundary clear while also expressing appreciation for James' intention. She recognizes that individuals have different comfort levels when it comes to sharing private details.

Over time, James adapts and keeps their conversations focused on less personal matters during work hours. Rather than crossing Samira's boundary again, he asks questions about her hobbies, favorite foods, and travels. Their rapport flourishes, grounded in mutual respect.

Samira also learns from this experience. In the future, she applies the same approach with other colleagues who pry into her off-work activities. She maintains her boundaries while also recognizing their perspective. Her calm, consistent enforcement of her boundaries combined with empathy for their intentions ultimately nurtures more positive work relationships.

In this way, respecting boundaries requires clarity, consistency, empathy and understanding from both parties.

For Samira, it involves clearly communicating her boundary while also considering her colleague's viewpoint. Rather than reacting angrily, she expresses her boundary in a measured way each time it is crossed. She also shows appreciation for James' intention to connect, even if it misses the mark.

For James, respecting Samira's boundary means listening to her feedback. Once he understands she prefers to separate her personal life from work interactions, he thoughtfully adapts his behavior. James also learns to get to know Samira through questions about her interests and experiences she feels comfortable discussing at work.

Additionally, respecting boundaries is an ongoing process. People's needs evolve, so there must be openness to gently renegotiate boundaries as comfort levels change on either side. Had life circumstances changed for Samira, she may have eventually felt ready to share more personal stories with trusted colleagues like James. As long as both parties communicate with empathy, boundaries can shift while still feeling safe.

The key is that boundaries are not about rejection or judgment. Even if James enjoys sharing his personal life at work, he accepts that Samira's needs differ. No one is inherently "right" or "wrong" - the goal is mutual understanding. With that spirit of empathy and compassion, honoring each other's boundaries strengthens workplace trust and respect.

Lastly, fostering relationships rooted in mutual respect and understanding also involves showing empathy and validation. It's about acknowledging the other person's feelings and experiences and validating them. This doesn't mean that you have to agree with everything they say or do, but simply acknowledging their feelings can go a long way in making them feel understood and valued.

Practice Scenario: Opening up about Personal Struggles in a Relationship

Let's move on to a practice scenario that will help us apply what we've learned about empathy, validation, and trust in relationships. This scenario involves a couple, Grace and Oliver, who are facing a challenging situation.

Grace and Oliver have been in a relationship for a few years. Recently, Oliver has been feeling overwhelmed with work and personal issues. He's been keeping these feelings to himself, not wanting to burden Grace. However, his stress has started to affect their relationship. He's become more withdrawn, and Grace has noticed this change.

One evening, Grace decides to address the issue. She approaches Oliver and expresses her concern about his recent behavior. She uses empathetic listening, validating his feelings, and expressing her willingness to support him. Feeling the trust and safety in their relationship, Oliver decides to open up about his struggles.

This case highlights the importance of empathy, validation, and trust in fostering open communication in relationships. It shows how these elements can encourage individuals to share their personal struggles, which ultimately leads to deeper connections.

Exercises and Reflection Points

Here I have provided some exercises and reflection points for you. These are designed to help you apply the concepts we've discussed in your own relationships. Remember, it's beneficial to journal your thoughts and reflections in a notebook. This practice can enhance your understanding and application of these concepts.

Exercises:

1. *Practice empathetic listening in your daily interactions.* Pay attention to not just what is being said but also the emotions and intentions behind the words.

2. *Practice expressing validation in your conversations.* This could be as simple as acknowledging the other person's feelings or perspective.

3. *Role-Play a Trust-Building Scenario*: With a partner, role-play a scenario where trust needs to be established or rebuilt. This could be a situation where one person has made

a mistake and needs to apologize and make amends. The other person should practice expressing their feelings and needs in a respectful and assertive manner.

4. *Role-Play a Difficult Conversation:* With a partner, role-play a challenging conversation where one person needs to express a personal struggle. The other person should practice empathetic listening and validation. Afterward, switch roles and repeat the exercise.

5. *Role-Play a Conflict Resolution:* In a group setting, role-play a scenario where a disagreement arises. Practice using empathy and validation to navigate the conflict and reach a resolution.

Reflection Points:

1. Reflect on a time when you felt truly heard and understood in a conversation. What made you feel this way? How did the other person demonstrate empathy and validation?

2. Think about a relationship where you feel a strong sense of trust. What behaviors or actions contribute to this trust?

3. Consider a situation where you had to open up about a personal struggle. How were empathy, validation, and trust involved in this process?

4. Reflect on your own level of openness and vulnerability during the role-play exercises. What factors made you feel safe or unsafe to express your personal struggles?

5. Reflect on the role-play exercises. How did it feel to prac-

tice empathetic listening and validation in these scenarios? What challenges did you encounter, and how did you overcome them?

6. Consider the role of trust in the role-play scenarios. How did the behaviors and actions of the 'characters' contribute to building or damaging trust?

Fostering relationships that are both vulnerable and fulfilling is an ever-evolving journey. It requires ongoing practice and reflection. As you continue to apply empathy, validation, and trust in your interactions, you'll be able to build deeper and more meaningful connections.

My Notes

Conclusion

Throughout our time in this book, we've navigated the intricate pathways of genuine human connection. We've highlighted the critical importance of empathy and validation in our relationships, pinpointing them as the key elements for building lasting bonds.

Being a beacon of empathy and validation means more than just understanding others. It's about opening up, being vulnerable, and actively listening. It's about recognizing that every person has a story, feelings, and experiences that deserve acknowledgment.

The pursuit of empathy and validation is more than just a personal endeavor; it's a collective movement towards a more conscious society that values understanding and compassion. By adopting the insights from this book, you're not only enhancing your ability to relate to others but also promoting a broader cultural change. The skills you've developed here are not just for personal benefit; they're essential for creating a more inclusive and understanding community.

We've painted a picture of a world where emotional connection is the norm, where every conversation is an opportunity to deepen our mutual understanding. In this world, empathy and validation are practiced daily.

As we wrap up, I want to express my sincere gratitude. Your commitment to this material, your engagement with the exercises, and your desire to understand empathy more deeply are truly commendable. People like you, who are proactive and eager to connect, are the driving force behind positive change.

Thank you for your time and effort. By applying these principles in your daily interactions, you're not only improving your relationships but also contributing to a more understanding world. Every act of kindness and understanding you show has a ripple effect. With individuals like you leading by example, our future looks promising, filled with genuine connections and mutual respect.

Acknowledgements

First and foremost, I would like to extend my heartfelt gratitude to all the individuals who have walked with me on this journey of understanding and articulating the profound concepts of empathy and emotional validation. Your stories, insights, and experiences have been the backbone of this work.

To my family and close friends, your unwavering support and belief in me have been the wind beneath my wings. Your patience and encouragement during the times I was immersed in research and writing have been invaluable.

A special thanks to my editor and the entire publishing team. Your expertise, feedback, and dedication have helped mold "The Power of Empathy and Emotional Validation" into the piece it is today.

And to you, dear reader, thank you for investing your time and energy in exploring the depths of human connection through these pages. I hope this book serves as a beacon, guiding you to richer, more empathetic relationships.

If this book resonated with you, I humbly ask for a small favor. Please consider leaving a review on Amazon. Your feedback not only helps me as an author but also aids potential readers in discovering the transformative power of empathy and emotional validation.

Thank you for being a part of this journey.

With warmth and gratitude,

Daniel Brooks

EXCLUSIVE BONUS: YOUR AUDIOBOOK AWAITS!

Dear valued reader,
We understand that life gets busy, and sometimes, you might not have the time to sit down with a book. As an exclusive bonus, we've created an audiobook version just for you! Now you can deepen your understanding of empathy and emotional validation on-the-go, anytime, anywhere.

Simply scan the QR code below to begin your audio journey to meaningful relationships and emotional intelligence.

About the Author

Daniel Brooks is a multifaceted communication coach, author, and counselor with over 15 years of experience in helping individuals unlock their full potential. He specializes in fostering empathy, emotional intelligence, and effective communication skills. Daniel's dedication to empowering individuals is evident in his transformative writings, where he combines insightful advice and personal anecdotes to guide readers toward deeper understanding and more meaningful relationships.

As a skilled communication coach, Daniel has worked with numerous individuals and teams to navigate complex conversations, fostering harmonious workplaces and personal relationships. His unique blend of empathy, humor, and practical guidance has solidified his reputation as a trusted advisor and mentor.

Outside of his professional pursuits, Daniel loves exploring the outdoors, traveling, and cherishing moments with his family.

References

I n this section, I have compiled a list of valuable sources and refer-
ences that have contributed to the understanding and knowledge
about empathy and emotional validation presented in this book.

- Goleman, D. (1999). Working with Emotional Intelligence.
  Bloomsbury Publishing PLC

- Claramicoli, A. and Ketcham, K. (2000). The Power of
  Empathy: A Practical Guide to Creating Intimacy, Self-understanding, and Lasting Love in Your Life. Dutton Adult

- Fuzzetti, A.E. (2006). The High-Conflict Couple: A Di-
  alectical Behavior Therapy Guide to Finding Peace, Intimacy, and Validation. New Harbinger Publications

- Perry, B.D. and Szalavits, M. (2011). Born for Love: Why
  Empathy Is Essential--and Endangered. William Morrow
  Paperbacks

- Miyashiro, M.R. (2011). The Empathy Factor: Your Com-
  petitive Advantage for Personal, Team, and Business Success. PuddleDancer Press

- Hall, K.D. and Cook, M. (2011). The Power of Validation:

Arming Your Child Against Bullying, Peer Pressure, Addiction, Self-Harm, and Out-of-Control Emotions. New Harbinger Publications

- McLaren, K. (2013). The Art of Empathy: A Complete Guide to Life's Most Essential Skill. Sounds True

- Krznaric, R. (2015). Empathy: Why It Matters, and How to Get It. TarcherPerigee

- Sorensen, M.S. (2017). I Hear You: The Surprisingly Simple Skill Behind Extraordinary Relationships. Autumn Creek Press

- Ventura, M. (2019). Applied Empathy: The New Language of Leadership. Atria

- Wright, E. (2021). The Art of Emotional Validation: Improve Your Communication Skills and Transform Your Relationships by Validating Emotions and Feelings. Bonus Liber

- King, P. (2021). How to Listen, Hear, and Validate: Break Through Invisible Barriers and Transform Your Relationships. Big Mind

- King, P. (2021). Intentional Communication: Emotional Validation, Listening, Empathy, and the Art of Harmonious Relationships. Big Mind

Printed in Great Britain
by Amazon

59858086R00097